Mastering the Router

A COMPLETE COURSE

99'11/22

Mastering the Router

A COMPLETE COURSE

Ron Fox

GUILD OF MASTER CRAFTSMAN PUBLICATIONS

This collection first published 2000 by
Guild of Master Craftsman Publications Ltd,
166 High Street, Lewes,
East Sussex, BN7 1XU

ISBN 1 86108 194 4
A catalogue record of this book is available from the British Library

Photographs by Anthony Bailey
Illustrations by Simon Rodway

Designed by Ed Le Froy
Cover design by Graham Willmott
Typeface: Frutiger

Printed and bound by Kyodo Printing (Singapore) under the supervision
of MRM Graphics, Winslow, Buckinghamshire, UK

NOTE

Every effort has been made to ensure that the information in this book
is accurate at the time of writing but inevitably prices, specifications,
and availability of tools will change from time to time. Readers are
therefore urged to contact manufacturers or suppliers for up-to-date
information before ordering tools.

CONTENTS

Introduction   1

Under starter's orders   2

At the cutting edge   6

Conditioning cutters   11

Get cutting   17

Beginner's luck   22

Clear cut   27

Holding the workpiece   32

Doctor depth   37

Under the table   43

In pursuit of clean living   49

Safety first   54

Kitting up for under £200   60

A guiding hand   67

Table chop   71

Guidebush buster   77

Routing free   82

Home help   88

On the edge   94

Routing a round   100

Working to a pattern   106

Fine cuts   111

Metric/Imperial conversion chart   118

About the author   119

Index   120

'Morning ducks.' Ron looks in on the manufacturing side of the family

INTRODUCTION

When *The Router* was in the planning stage I received, out of the blue, an invitation from Paul Richardson to contribute articles for the 'Beginner's Guide' series. At the time I was into my fourth year of giving routing courses, aimed mainly at the beginner on a one-to-one basis, and had formed some clear ideas as to the needs of the complete newcomer to routing. I accepted Paul's invitation on the spot and have been contributing ever since without, so far, missing an issue.

It is hard to believe that over three years have gone by since the first issue of the magazine. During those years a considerable number of new – and newly-badged – routers and cutters have appeared, along with other items of equipment, but the principles and techniques of routing have not changed.

My experience of giving courses on a one-to-one basis, plus the opportunities I have had to discuss routing with hundreds of visitors to some of the major exhibitions, has led me to appreciate the degree of detail in which the beginner needs to have matters explained. The articles, therefore, set out to help with the things that loom large when first taking up routing. First and foremost is the question of what router to buy. The usual response is 'What do you want to do with it?', but until someone knows all the things that a router is capable of, they may not know what they want to do with it. I have therefore tried to cover most of the things that can be done with a router – not all of them very obvious – in order to provide a sensible basis for selection.

The next most obvious area is the selection of cutters. There is an absolutely bewildering variety available these days and cutters can easily become the bottomless pit of routing expenditure, though this does not have to be the case. Careful selection and maintenance of a limited set of cutters can fulfil most of one's needs, and the ability to keep cutters sharp with a diamond hone enables budget-priced cutters to perform more than adequately for most 'domestic' projects.

I hope that this book will encourage the reader to have a go rather than just dream about doing so. Among the merits of power tools in general, and the router in particular, is the fact that the amateur can get good results in a relatively short time and the 'weekend woodworker', whose greatest problem is time, can start and finish a simple project without having to put it away, incomplete, until time next becomes available.

Apart from the first two, these articles were written as practical work sessions. I hope that all who read and work through them learn something from each, as I have done in their writing.

Under start

Looking at the router's main components

WITH the appropriate cutter and perhaps a suitable jig or attachment, the router can perform almost every woodworking operation. In subsequent chapters I will be examining how this versatile tool can perform so many different tasks, but I'll kick off by describing its main components and analysing the factors to be considered when choosing one.

Components
The modern plunge router consists of three main components:

■ High-speed motor, often with variable speed;

■ Collet on the end of the motor spindle to hold a fixed-diameter cutter shank;

■ Pair of sprung columns, fixed to a base plate, which carry the motor in its housing and allow the cutter to be plunged to a predetermined depth.

Motor
Motor power determines the range of operations that can be undertaken. A rough classification of power rating is 400–600W for light duty models, 750–1100W for medium duty and 1300–2000W for heavy duty.

These are input figures, output power being about 60% of input. All but the smallest DIY routers are offered with a variable-speed version. This opens up a much wider range of applications and goes particularly with high power.

High power means you can use large-diameter cutters. Because these create very

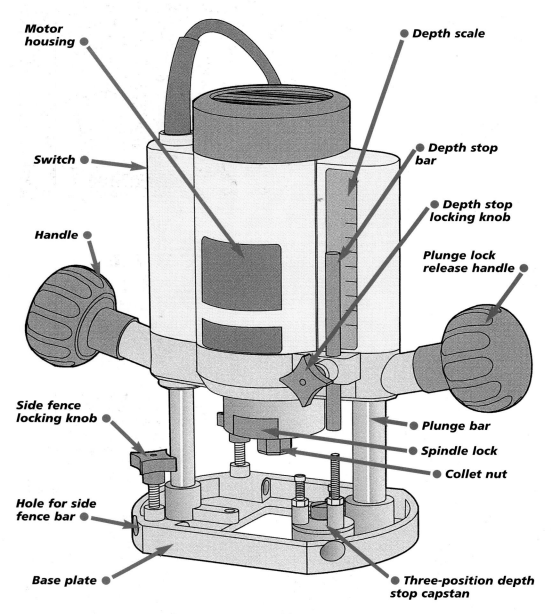

- Motor housing
- Switch
- Handle
- Side fence locking knob
- Hole for side fence bar
- Base plate
- Depth scale
- Depth stop bar
- Depth stop locking knob
- Plunge lock release handle
- Plunge bar
- Spindle lock
- Collet nut
- Three-position depth stop capstan

▲ **Parts of a router**

high peripheral speeds, motor speed must therefore be reduced accordingly.

Fixed-speed routers operate at up to 30,000rpm and variable-speed models at between 8,000 and 26,000rpm.

While you need enough power to meet your requirements, the benefit of high power for such things as table routing has to be balanced against a heavy, bulky machine when it comes to freehand work.

Collet

The collet corresponds to the chuck in a drill, and is made to take one specific shank size. As it is the vital link between the cutter and a motor turning at up to 30,000rpm, it pays to choose a router with a well-engineered collet.

The best come in multi-slot tempered steel, shaped to fit in a corresponding taper in the motor spindle.

Light-duty routers have only ¼in collets. Most medium power routers are supplied with ¼in collets, but with an 8mm collet as an accessory. Heavy-duty routers are usually supplied with ½in and ¼in collets, but some come with reducing sleeves for the smaller sizes.

Proper sized collets are the better option.

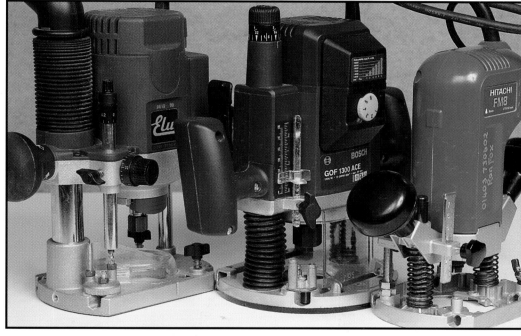

▲ *Different kinds of depth-setting control*

Plunge legs

These allow the cutter to be plunged to the desired depth of cut. The base plate carries the legs and ensures that the cutter is presented to the work at a precise right-angle – making an excellent drilling machine as well.

The plunge legs are locked at the desired height by means of a locking lever on the body of the router or by twisting one of the handles. A

few routers have spring-loaded plunge-lock levers which have to be pressed to release the lock.

Base plate

This is the part that makes contact with the workpiece, so it must be flat, friction-free, tough and replaceable. A removable Tufnol or plastic facing plate, and threaded holes for attach-

"If the collet can be plunged to touch the bench top you can't really complain; anything deeper than that is a bonus"

ing work aids or mounting the router in a table, are fundamental requirements.

Some DIY routers have no facing plate, their metal bases being simply finished with paint or anodised.

Good visual access through the base plate is essential. Some routers have tiny apertures which make it difficult to see what you are doing, a matter made even worse if a dust extraction spout is fitted.

This is no problem when using guidebushes or bearing-guided cutters, since such work is done largely by

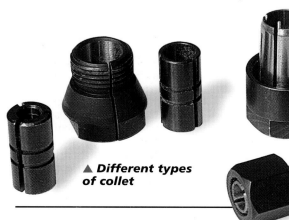

▲ *Different types of collet*

Buying checklist

Motor and power
What is your intended use?
Light DIY, furniture and similar? Variable speed provides greater flexibility.

Size and weight
What is your intended use?
Table/heavy cutting, finer and lighter cutting, free-hand work?

Collets – Look at quality and range available, avoid reducing sleeves.

Depth of cut – Is the depth sufficient for use in tables and with guidebushes?

Depth of cut adjustment – How precise is it? Is it easy to set up and use?

Handles and switches – Are they easy to use and accessible?

Base plate – Has it got fittings for table use, guidebushes and other attachments? Check visibility.

Side fence – Is it well made, with good fittings and bars for other attachments?

Dust extraction – Are the fittings of good quality? Do they obscure visibility?

Table use – The ideal router for table use should have a base plate with good visibility, substantial attachment points, a deep-plunging collet, a simple switch – even if operated via an NVR switch – and a fine height adjuster for easy and accurate depth setting.

▲ *A small selection of the routers on the market available for beginners*

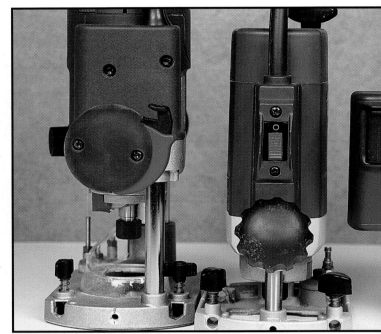

▲ *Switches vary from simple to complicated*

touch, but the more common tasks, such as grooving using the side fence, are made difficult if you cannot see to set the fence.

Depth control

Factors to consider here are how precisely and easily the cut can be set, and what provision there is on the fine adjuster to prevent the router rising if the plunge lock is inadvertently released.

A fine adjuster is a great convenience in setting the exact depth of cut, and a rise limiter is a valuable safety measure when dovetailing.

With nearly all makes – except for the smallest models – a rotating turret provides three different plunge stops for one setting of the bar.

Most routers use a form of vertical sliding bar set against a built-in scale, and clamped in position. While some of the latest models have the fine adjuster built in, others have it as an accessory.

Depth of cut

Some models lose depth of cut because their plunging mechanism does not allow the collet to reach the work surface.

Such models are at a disadvantage when used in a router table or with a template and guidebush because depth of cut is lost through the thickness of the table insert or template.

If the collet can be plunged to touch the bench top you can't really complain; anything deeper than that is a bonus and anything much shorter could create problems with certain applications.

Handles

Handle versions are either twist knob or side lever. Many light- and medium-duty models incorporate the switch or plunge-lock control in one of the handles.

Heavy-duty routers invariably have side-lever handles for maximum leverage, with switch and plunge lock located elsewhere.

Switch

The switch can have a profound effect on ease of use, and the rule is, the simpler the better.

But due to safety regulations, however, simple slide

"Most beginners are looking for the best combination of capability, versatility and portability"

▲ **Standard accessories supplied with routers**

switches are rare, with complicated latching systems or 'dead man's handle' types becoming increasingly common.

With the latter the switch has to be clipped or strapped 'ON' if the router is used in a table. This is a nuisance and could be dangerous unless a no-volt release (NVR) switch is fitted to the router table.

Dust extraction

Most routers come with an extractor spout either as standard or as an accessory. One or two models incorporate built-in extraction ports. Some extractor spouts can inhibit visibility.

Side fence

A substantial fence with removable rods, and holes for fitting a false wooden fence, is desirable. Fences on most routers, apart from DIY models, feature fine adjusters which come into the "how did I ever do without it" category.

The benefit of removable rods is that they can be used with other accessories. For the same reason, long rods are better than short ones.

As standard

Most routers are supplied with a number of accessories, commonly a side fence and guidebush, and often a plastic dust extractor spout.

Guidebushes

Put a high value on a good range of guidebushes. They should preferably fit into the router without the need for a centring device.

Fortunately it is nearly always possible to make or buy an auxiliary base plate to take another manufacturer's guidebushes if your model lacks its own.

Which model?

Never buy solely on price. By the time you have bought cutters, perhaps a dovetail jig, maybe a router table etc., the cost of the router will be a relatively minor part of your total expenditure.

The ability to make the best use of additional equipment will be more important than the initial outlay.

Begin by deciding what you want the router for. If it is primarily for toymaking or small cabinets you will not want a high-powered heavy-

▲ **A basic guidebush is supplied as standard**

▲ **Some routers are supplied with a dust extractor spout, others have them built in**

weight that will be cumbersome for intricate hand work. Conversely, light-duty DIY models will be inadequate if you plan to refurbish your home.

Between these extremes, most beginners are looking for the best combination of capability, versatility and portability (*see checklist panel on page 4*).

In addition

The versatility of the router depends not only on the range of accessories offered by its manufacturer but also on its suitability for use with other suppliers' products. So consider what other equip-

ment you might aspire to, and its suitability for use with your proposed router.

For example, dovetailing involves heavy cuts; as you cannot take incremental light cuts with a dovetail cutter, a router of at least 900W is indicated.

No one router will score full marks on all the features, so list your requirements in order of priority and select the model accordingly.

At the cutting edge

Looking at cutters

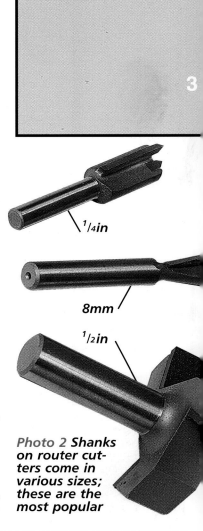

The versatility of the router is due in very large part to the bewilderingly vast range of cutters available for it. The purpose of this chapter is to pick a way through the maze, identifying the essential cutters needed to get started.

Cutter materials

The two most common materials for router cutters are high-speed steel (HSS) and tungsten-carbide-tipped (TCT).

HSS cutters are less expensive than TCT and can be honed to a razor-sharp edge. Unfortunately this edge wears rapidly and has to be maintained by frequent honing. HSS cutters give the best results with natural timbers.

TCT cutters can't take such a keen edge as HSS cutters, but hold it much longer. They can also cut chipboard and other manufactured boards which would quickly ruin an HSS cutter.

Unless you plan to double up on your cutters – HSS for natural wood, TCT for manufactured boards and tough hardwoods – the choice comes down to TCT.

Cutters can be divided into broad groups according to their function.

GROUP 1
Straight

These are the workhorse cutters with which most of the basic woodworking operations are carried out, including cutting, grooving, rebating and making joints.

Diameters larger than 6mm should preferably have centre-cutting inserts to facilitate plunging, but most budget-priced examples do not.

GROUP 2
Trimming

These are straight cutters with bearings of the same diameter as the cutter, mounted either on a spigot at the bottom of the cutter or on the shank immediately above the cutter.

They are useful for trimming boards to exact length, for repetitive cutting of shapes using a pattern, and for trimming lippings and laminates.

GROUP 3
Shaping

These are used for producing the decorative edges and panels for which the router is renowned. They come in a vast number of shapes and sizes, often with rather strange names taken from architecture, like astragal, bolection, ogee, ovolo, pilaster etc.

Photo 2 Shanks on router cutters come in various sizes; these are the most popular

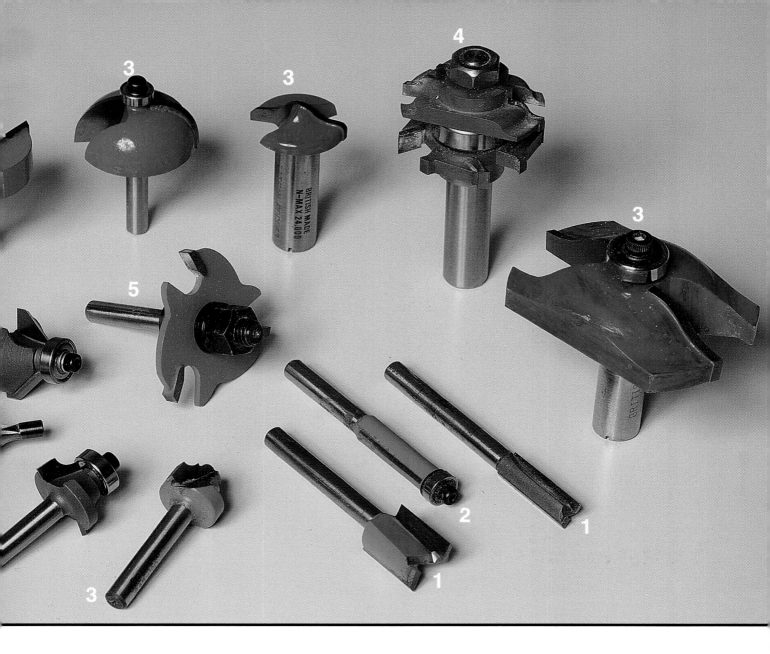

Photo 1 *The versatility of the router is mainly due to the vast range of cutters available: Group 1, straight cutters; Group 2, trimming cutter; Group 3, shaping cutters; Group 4, jointing cutter; Group 5, arbor-mounted cutters*

Many of them are fitted with a bearing to guide the cutter.

GROUP 4
Jointing

These are specialised cutters for producing joints such as dovetails, finger joints, glue joints and mitre joints. Many are large, requiring heavy-duty routers with ¹/₂in shanks, and must be used in a router table at a reduced speed.

GROUP 5
Arbor-mounted

These are cutters mounted on an arbor to act rather like miniature circular saws. The best known examples are the slotters used for biscuit jointing, rebates and tongue-and-groove joints, where more than one slotter can be mounted on the arbor so as to make the cut in one pass.

As with the jointing cutters,

Photo 3 *A selection of different types of collet*

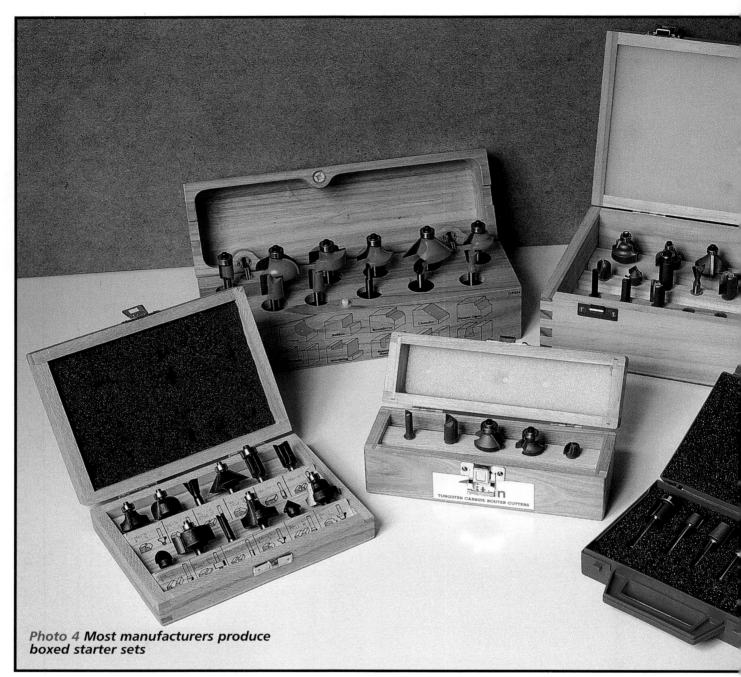

Photo 4 Most manufacturers produce boxed starter sets

some require a ¹/₄in shank arbor mounted in a heavy-duty router.

Shank diameter

The majority of routers in use in the UK are made to take ¹/₄in shank cutters. Heavy-duty routers have ¹/₂in collets but usually include a ¹/₄in collet or reducing sleeve.The larger the diameter of the shank the stronger the cutter will be, so if you have a ¹/₂in router you should aim to use ¹/₂in shank cutters wherever possible.

A recent development in the UK is the introduction of cutters on 8mm shanks. An 8mm shank has about 60% more cross-sectional area than a ¹/₄in shank.

Not only does this give a better cut, with higher feed rates, but it opens up the prospect of a range of heavier, more diverse cutters than is available on ¹/₄in shanks.

Boxed starter sets

Boxed starter sets offer the advantage of a number of cutters with which to explore the potential of the router at about half the price of the same cut-

ters bought separately.

They vary from six to 22 cutters, but a typical set of 12 would include three or four straight cutters, three or four bearing-guided moulding cutters, a flush trimming cutter, V-groover and dovetail cutter, with a pierce-and-trim, or core box, or rebater.

Most boxed sets contain budget-priced cutters, although those from CMT and Freud,

plus two industrial sets from Titman, consist of premium grade ones and are priced accordingly.

All are TCT, although the better-quality sets might include one

Photo 5 Complex mouldings can be made by using more than one cutter

"A recent development in the UK is the introduction of cutters on 8mm shanks"

round-over to an ovolo.

Cutters can also be used in combination to produce complex mouldings, taking several passes on the same piece of wood with, for example, a straight followed by an ovolo followed by a core box cutter.

It pays to compare very carefully the make-up of all the sets available before finally choosing.

While budget-priced starter sets might not be of industrial grade, they offer the beginner an attractive way to get started, subsequent cutters being bought individually as experience and need dictate.

Boxed sets on ¼in shanks are available from Axminster Power Tools, BJR, Charnwood, CMT, Freud, KWO, Titan, Titman, Trend and Wealden, to name but a few. Heavier-duty sets on ½in shanks are available from most of these companies.

Inevitably in any set selected by the manufacturer there may be several that get little use.

Single cutters
An equally valid approach is to buy cutters individually for specific purposes. The costs will be slightly more per cutter, but exactly the right cutters will be obtained.

My own starter set would include 6, 10, 13 and 16mm straight cutters, a 13mm flush-trimmer with a cut length of 25mm, a Roman ogee, a round-over with a second bearing to give an ovolo, a V-groover for practising freehand control of the router, and a 4mm slotter on an arbor for biscuit jointing.

If I was catering for a ½in router I would also buy a 6mm straight on a ¼in shank because you cannot properly hone a 6mm cutter on a ½in shank.

or two solid carbide cutters. Not surprisingly, ¼in shanks are more readily available than ½in shanks.

Suppliers are now offering boxed sets with 8mm shanks.

Varied uses
In practice you get more than the actual number of cutters in the box because, for example, moulding cutters such as the Roman ogee can be used at less than full depth to vary the shape of the cut, and if the set contains cutters with different diameter bearings, these can be interchanged to convert, say, a

Care of cutters

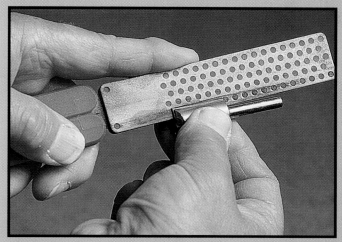

Photo 7 *A keen cutting edge can be produced by using a diamond hone*

Frequent cleaning and honing will keep your cutters in first-class condition.

Dirty cutters result in excess heat on the cutting edges which dulls them.

Resinous deposits can be removed with a solvent such as lighter fuel or, better still, contact adhesive remover. For more stubborn deposits use a mild abrasive cleaner such as 'Astonish' and a little elbow grease. With bearing-guided cutters, remove the bearings before cleaning to avoid washing out their lubricant.

After cleaning, hone the flat faces of the cutter using a diamond hone with a few drops of water on the surface. The best is the red-

coloured all-round 'Fine' grade.

Make certain that the cutter face is absolutely flat on the hone and rub it firmly backwards and forwards. Give each face the same number of strokes. Both HSS and TCT cutters respond to the diamond hone.

After honing, the cutter should be given a squirt of lubricant spray such as WD40 or PTFE.

Finally, dry the surface of the hone and clean it with a plastic eraser. Trend make a cutter and collet care kit which includes an instructional booklet.

To have a cutter reground contact your local saw doctor; you will find them in your Yellow Pages.

Photo 6 *An ideal set can be created with cutters bought individually*

Good light and total concentration to hone a razor-sharp edge on the cutter

Conditioning cutters

Keeping your cutters in trim

NEWCOMERS to routing soon find the investment in cutters quickly exceeds that in the original router.

It makes sense to plan your cutter-buying strategy carefully, and to keep cutters in top condition.

Fortunately, cutter maintenance is a very simple matter. Keep them clean and keep them sharp. Store them safely in a way that prevents corrosion and stops them rattling against each other.

I will be looking at tungsten-carbide-tipped (TCT) cutters, but the methods can be applied to high-speed steel (HSS) cutters.

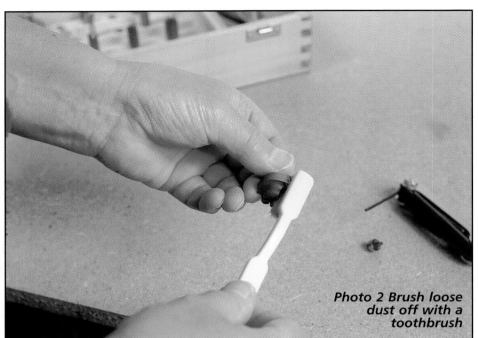

Photo 2 Brush loose dust off with a toothbrush

Cutter cleaning

A clean cutter is halfway to a sharp cutter, and the sharper the cutter the cleaner the cuts. The burnt deposits that accumulate on the edge of a cutter, and the film of resin from the material being cut, heat up when using the cutter again. The build-up of heat on the edge of the cutter blade does as much to dull the cutting edge as the abrasive nature of the material being worked.

Begin by removing the bearings from any bearing-guided cutters to be cleaned. This gives access to all parts of the cutter, and avoids washing away the bearing lubricant with solvent.

Brush off all loose dust with an old toothbrush. A more abrasive brush such as a 'Hush Puppy' suede brush or a spark plug brush could be used, but this isn't necessary as any deposits that remain are removed with solvent.

After brushing there are likely to be traces of resin or burned deposits on the cutter. Remove these resin deposits with a dab of solvent on a rag.

The best solvent I have come across for this purpose is the one made for removing excess contact adhesive when laminating with Formica etc. Unfortunately this solvent is no longer found on the open shelves in shops; you have to ask for it. I buy mine from the local ironmonger.

Any solvent you have handy is worth trying. Trend package a specific resin remover, and other solvents with names like 'Sticky Stuff Remover' are available.

WD40 is quite good as a resin remover as

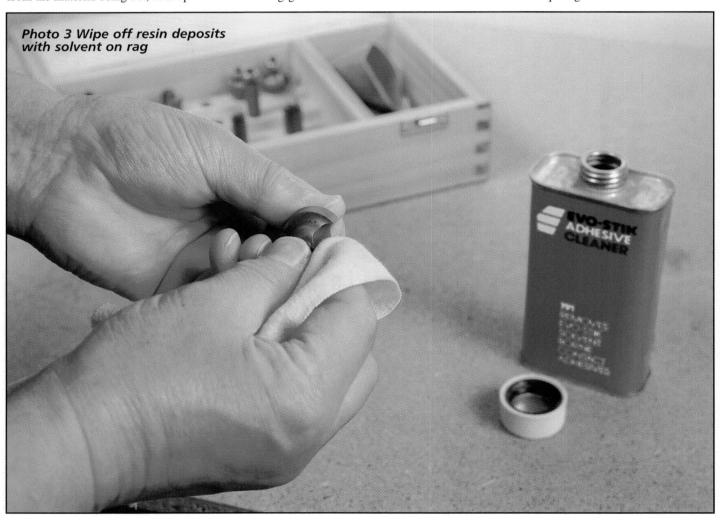

Photo 3 Wipe off resin deposits with solvent on rag

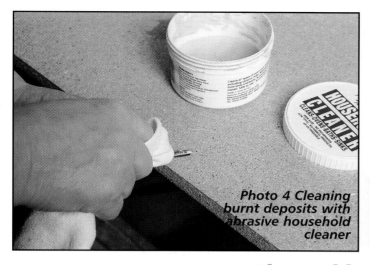

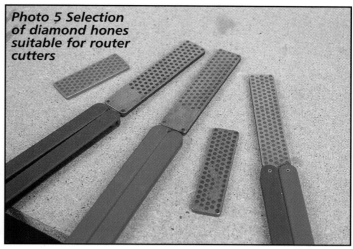

Photo 5 Selection of diamond hones suitable for router cutters

Photo 4 Cleaning burnt deposits with abrasive household cleaner

well as a lubricant, but I have not come across anything to beat the contact adhesive remover.

Solvent

Most cutters will be clean after the brush and solvent treatment, but if you have been working with chipboard or really tough hardwood you may have heavier burnt deposits that won't yield to the solvent.

For these, a household abrasive cleaner and a bit of elbow grease will do the job. The cleaner I use is called 'Astonish', but there are various other brands on the market, any of which are worth a try.

Follow these steps and your cutters will look like new. Any cutter that doesn't respond to this treatment is probably beyond repair. Bin it.

Finally, wipe your cutters dry and spray them with silicone, WD40 or any similar spray. The current favourite seems to be one of the PTFE-based sprays. Spraying has two benefits:

1. It prevents corrosion from the solvent or damp rag
2. The spray lubricates the next time you use the cutter. When the spray dries it allows the cutter to run a little cooler and cleaner. To some extent this delays the build-up of further deposits. This is why a clean cutter is halfway to a sharp cutter.

Diamond hones

After cleaning you can refresh the edges of your cutters with a diamond hone. This is what has transformed the maintenance of TCT cutters. Before the advent of the thin diamond-plate hone it simply was not possible.

Most makes adopt the same colour-coding system: green is extra fine; red is fine; blue is coarse and black is extra coarse.

The hones come in a range of sizes, from a small slip stone to a flat bench stone. Router cutters need a thin one, and my favourite is the 4in folding-handle type.

The next most useful is the 3in plain kind, which can be taped to a bench top.

Different grades

A recent addition to the hone market is the Double Diafold from DMT. Three versions are available: extra fine/fine, fine/coarse, and coarse/extra coarse. They cost little more than a single grade. The fine/coarse is needed for router cutters.

Normal honing is done on the fine-grade plate, with the coarse one in reserve to bring back a cutter that has got blunter than intended, finished with a few strokes on the fine side.

It is important to recognise that we are honing our cutters, not grinding them. This means applying the hone 'little and often', rather than waiting until the cutter is blunt and trying to restore it.

Imagine an old-fashioned barber and his razor; he never picks it up without giving it a few strokes on his strop.

Wet surface

To use the hone, wet the surface of the diamond plate with water, bed the flat face of the cutting blade on the surface of the stone and rub it back and forth.

Keep the plate well wetted. Only light pressure is needed – let the diamond do the work. Repeat for the other edges, giving each edge the same number of strokes to preserve the balance of the cutter.

With HSS cutters a very slight burr might be formed, but I haven't come across this with a TCT cutter. Remove the burr with a gentle stroke on the back of the cutting edge.

The crucial question is, how many strokes do we need to give the edge? Basically, as many as it needs. You will be the judge of that; you will have other cutters – perhaps some still unused – to give you an original edge for reference.

Cutters with broad faces are the easiest to start with but, in general, straight cutters are quite simple until you come down to a ¼in cutter on ¼in shank. At this point it is impossible to lay the cutting edge with the shank parallel to the hone. It is also difficult to ensure the very narrow flat face is bedded on the diamond plate.

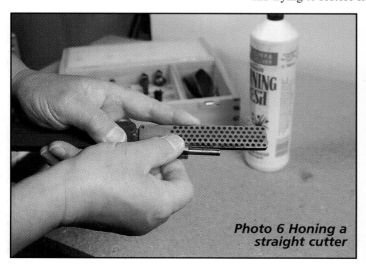

Photo 6 Honing a straight cutter

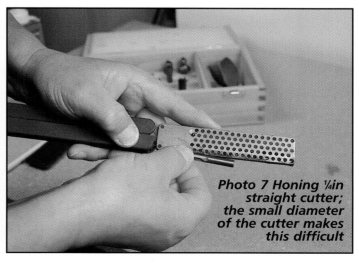

Photo 7 Honing ¼in straight cutter; the small diameter of the cutter makes this difficult

Photo 8 Honing a cutter with hone held on bench top

can never be honed, the spiral for example, and here the same applies.

Hand-held honing allows you to change angles to ensure the cutter face is properly bedded on the diamond plate. You may find it more efficient to hold or tape the hone to the edge of the bench top and work in the manner shown.

Bearing-guided cutters

The bearing-guided cutter often perplexes the beginner, as some assume it cannot be honed, but with the bearing removed you will find these are among the easiest to hone.

It's important to ignore the angle the cutter shank makes with the diamond plate. Different cutters have the blades set at different angles; any attempt to hold the shank level with the edge of the hone will cause the cutter edge to round over.

Finally, clean the hone and make sure it's dry before putting it away. The easiest way to clean the surface of the diamond plate is to rub it with a plastic eraser.

Regular maintenance will prolong your cutter's life, but eventually you might want to have a cutter professionally re-sharpened.

Titman's recommend sending your cutters to a member of the Saw Doctors Association, to ensure a proper standard of service. You will find the name of your local members in your Yellow Pages.

Some woodworkers choose to have more than one ¼in cutter, keeping one for their best cabinet work, letting it 'grow old gracefully', then sending it for re-grinding, while keeping another for everyday work and honing it as best they can.

Shanks

When the cutter becomes narrower than the shank, e.g. a 4mm cutter on a ¼in shank, honing becomes impractical. Just keep the cutter clean and sprayed, sending it for re-sharpening if it is economical. Some cutters

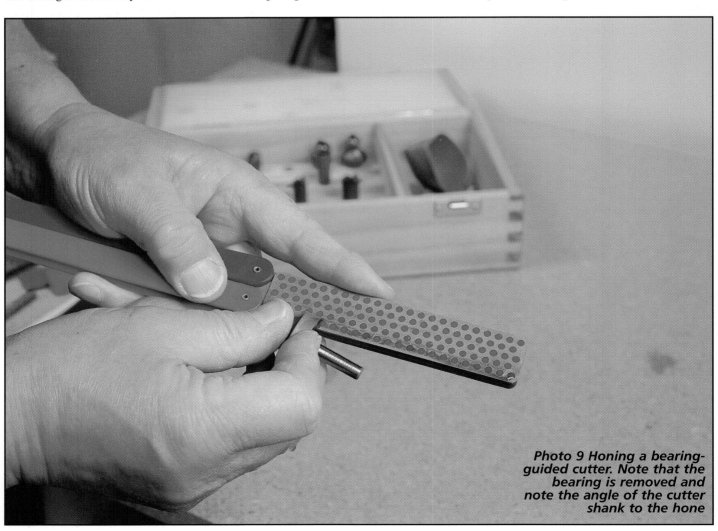

Photo 9 Honing a bearing-guided cutter. Note that the bearing is removed and note the angle of the cutter shank to the hone

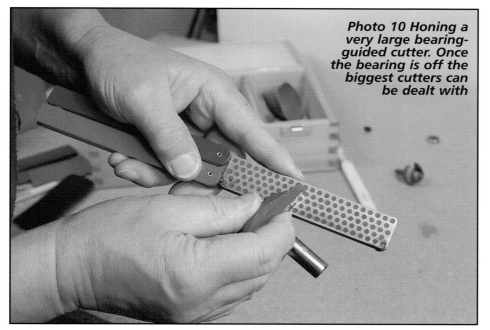

Photo 10 Honing a very large bearing-guided cutter. Once the bearing is off the biggest cutters can be dealt with

Cutter storage

Having freshly sharpened your cutters they need to be stored safely. If part of a boxed set this isn't a problem. Keep them in their box and spray the shanks and heads so they don't corrode from contact with the box. This is particularly important if the cutters are stored in damp or humid conditions. Most boxes now incorporate plastic inserts so the cutter shanks don't touch the wood. Squirt a few drops of lubricant into these inserts to protect the shanks and also ease their removal.

Individual cutters come in various forms of packaging; plastic envelopes, or boxes, and elaborate cases with a plastic bobbin in the base to hold the shank.

If the packaging is poor, use a block of wood to take the shanks. You can make the block a more finished looking item by moulding the edges.

Use softwood or a very mild hard wood for your cutter block – the chemical, tannin, that is present in a block of green oak turns the shanks of your cutters blue. If you make a block, drill holes big enough to give clearance to the shank. For ½in shanks I use a 13mm twist drill. This reduces the possibility of corrosion from contact with the wood and might save your fingers from a nasty cut trying to pull a tight cutter out of the block.

Collet maintenance

Since cutters are fitted into collets, their maintenance is important too. The collet is one of the few parts of the router that needs regular care and attention.

The basic job is to keep the collet, motor spindle and collet housing clean. Remove dust with a dental brush or the set of brass brushes included in the Trend Cutter and Collet Care Kit.

Photo 11 Spraying a cutter after honing

▲ *Photo 12 Cleaning hone with a plastic eraser*

▲ *Photo 13 Cutters stored in boxes, blocks of wood and original plastic cases*

Remove resins and gums in the same way as for cutters, and once cleaned, inspect the collet for signs of wear.

The two most common forms of wear are 'belling' at each end of the collet, and stress marks or scratches on the internal collet faces.

If these signs are obvious, consider replacing the collet. They are ultimately expendable items. A worn collet will cause poor cutting, possibly ruin the shanks of your cutters and even worse, the cutter may slip out. It is cheaper and safer to replace the collet before this happens.

If your collet is of the multi-slit 'thimble'

type e.g. DeWalt 625, Trend T9, Trend T5, Perles etc., the thimble can be removed from the collet nut for cleaning and inspection.

Do make sure you spring the thimble back into the collet nut before screwing the nut back on to the motor shaft. If you don't the collet will not be pulled out of the motor shaft when you loosen the nut to remove the cutter.

Remember: never use the router without the collet firmly sprung into its nut.

Multi-slits

Cleaning multi-slit thimble collets is made slightly complicated because some

manufacturers, such as Bosch, fit collets of the same highly efficient multi-slit type, but the 'thimble' is fixed into the nut with a spring ring. If you ever replace one it will come complete with collet nut.

Other manufacturers are beginning to follow Bosch's example; for example, the collets for the DeWalt DW621 are now fixed into their nuts and sold as a complete unit.

Finally, Trend publish a very good little book, *Cutter and Collet Care*, which is well worth reading.

Photo 14 Cleaning a ¼in collet with a dental brush. Note Trend brass brushes in picture

Get cutting

Starting to use your cutters

Having looked at which router and cutter to choose (*see pages 2–9*), we can now consider how to position the cut. This is, literally, a two-dimensional problem: the vertical, or depth of cut, and the horizontal, or distance from the edge of the workpiece.

We'll look at cutting a rebate along the edge of a workpiece, a cut used when setting the back into a cabinet or for taking the glass in a window frame or cabinet door. We shall make the cut with a ⅝in straight cutter guided by the router's side fence.

Setting depth

The procedure for setting depth of cut is as follows:-

1. Install the cutter, inserting about three-quarters of the shank length into the collet and tightening the nut firmly but without any white-knuckle stuff.

2. If the router has a rotating turret, set it so that the shortest stop screw is immediately below the stop bar.

3. Plunge the router until the cutter just rests on the workpiece.

4. Lower the stop bar until it is resting on the stop screw or, in the absence of a turret, the router base; this procedure varies according to router models.

5. Raise the stop bar a distance equal to the required depth of cut; with DIY models measuring this gap can be awkward, but the problem is easily overcome in one of two ways:

a. Use a twist drill as a feeler gauge. For a 10mm cut, place the shank of a 10mm twist drill between the stop bar and the stop

▲ *Depth-setting mechanisms vary on different brands of router but they all do the same job*

▲ Plunge the router so that the cutter just touches the surface of the workpiece

▲ Rotate the turret so that the shortest stop screw is below the stop bar, then drop the bar to it

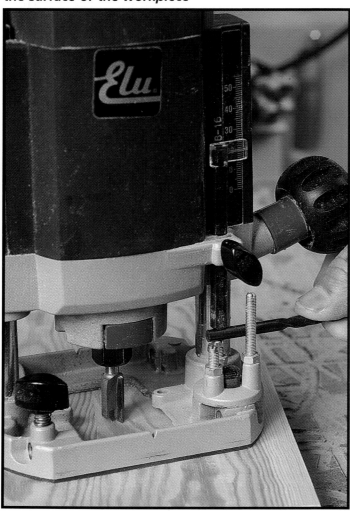

▲ To set the depth of cut, place a drill bit of a known diameter between the stop bar and stop screw

▲ An alternative way to set the depth of cut is to use a vernier gauge

Use the eyeball method to set the depth of cut on bearing-guided cutters. Their distance from an edge is pre-determined by the bearing

"Fine adjusters either replace or supplement the normal depth-setting system"

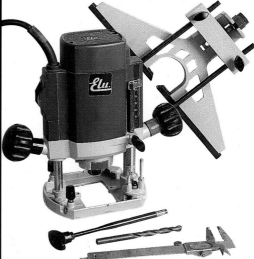

▲ Fine adjusters on the depth stop and side fence make life easier when setting up; some routers are supplied with them while others offer them as accessories

screw or router base. Other feeler gauges can be accumulated from scraps of various materials of known thickness.

b. Use a vernier gauge – available from DIY superstores for around £2.50. Set the gauge to the depth of 10mm and insert the two external prongs between the stop bar and the stop, lowering and locking the stop bar to give the depth of cut.

More sophisticated routers have the equivalent of the vernier gauge built in to the depth-setting device. Having lowered the stop bar to the stop screw, the setting is put to zero and the stop bar wound up by the required amount, reading off a built-in scale.

Having set the final depth of cut, the other turret screws can be set to give intermediate depths so that, for example, our 10mm cut can be made in two 5mm passes, the first with the intermediate position of the turret, the second with the final position.

Bearing guided

The above procedures do not apply to bearing-guided cutters because the bearing and Allen screw prevent these being plunged to the work surface.

When edge moulding with this kind of cutter, the usual procedure is to set the full depth of cut by eye with the cutter against the edge of the workpiece; lock the stop bar

and use the intermediate positions of the turret to accomplish three light cuts.

If the router has no turret the first cut can be set by eye and the second by reference to the stop bar, leaving a small gap – say 2mm – between stop bar and router. The final cut is then made by plunging to the original setting; the small gap left when setting the second cut ensures that the third and final cut is very light, producing the best possible finish.

Height adjusters

Setting depth of cut is essentially a question of accurately setting the stop bar, but a number of routers provide additional fine adjustment, either built in as in the Bosch 900/1300 series, or as accessories as in the Elu 96/97/177 (DeWalt 613/621/625) series.

These fine adjusters either replace or supplement the normal depth-setting system and work on the principle of a threaded rod linking the router body and base. This lowers the cutter as it is tightened and raises it as it is loosened.

Such adjusters enable the depth of cut to be set and held with precision, provide a means of setting depth of cut when the router is inverted in a table, and act as a valuable safety measure against accidentally releasing the plunge lock, so allowing a

rotating cutter to come up through the guidebush – disastrous when dovetailing.

Edge distance

Our example is a rebate along the edge of the workpiece, and to achieve similar cuts, such as grooves set in from the edge, we use the router's side fence. The side fence is often referred to as a 'straight' or 'parallel guide'.

All but the small DIY models now come with fences incorporating a fine adjuster. These allow a 'coarse' setting to be made by means of the fence rods and their clamping screws, followed by a fine setting using the adjuster.

As with depth of cut we will take the setting of the fence in stages:-

1. Mark the line of cut with a gauge or pencil.

2. Place the router, fitted with the side fence, on the workpiece with the cutter blades in the 'east–west' position relative to the edge of the work; align the inner blade with the line of cut and tighten the fence rod clamping screws; if your fence has no fine adjuster, check that tightening the clamping screws has not shifted the position of the fence, and repeat the operation until satisfied.

3. If your fence has a fine adjuster, slacken the clamping screws and turn the adjust-

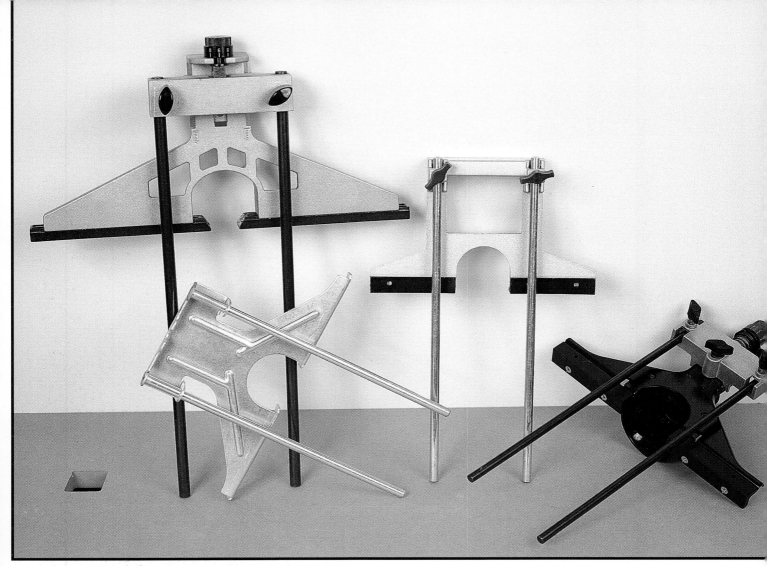

▲ *An array of side fences with and without fine adjusters*

ing knob to move the cutter blade in or out to the exact line of cut. Tighten the clamping screws and check (*see step 2*). Do not slacken the clamping screws more than necessary or the fence will sag and the setting will be slightly out when tightened.

Note: the accuracy of your cut depends as much on the 'east–west' positioning of your cutter blades as it does on the fence adjustment, so make a test cut and reset as necessary.

Grooved cuts

A similar procedure is followed to cut a groove or surface decoration parallel to the edge of the workpiece for mortices, fluting on fireplace surrounds and grooving for inlaid banding.

As with depth of cut, bearing-guided cutters do not follow the above rules. The bearing on the cutter takes the place of the fence in guiding the cut, and controls the position of the cut relative to the edge of the workpiece.

The bearing will follow a straight or curved edge.

The precision with which depth of cut and distance from the edge can be set has improved remarkably in recent years. With some professional models, however, the fine depth adjuster is still an optional extra. I regard it as an essential.

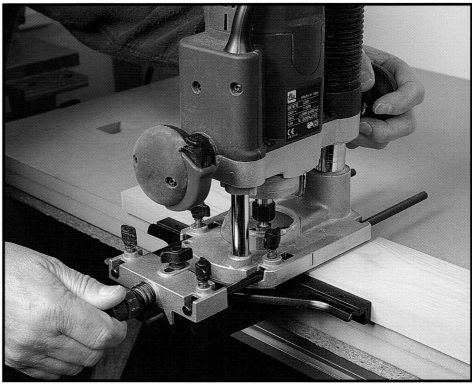

▲ *Use the side fence to set a rebate cut or a groove. A fine adjuster, if fitted, will give greater accuracy*

Ron explaining the subtleties of the run-in/run-out problem

Beginner's luck

Avoiding common problems

THE router is sufficiently unlike other power tools to present a number of new, and possibly unexpected, problems to the beginner. Here we examine some of the more common ones.

> ## "Many beginners do not realise that there is a right and wrong direction of cut when using a router"

Direction of cut

Many beginners do not realise that there is a right and a wrong direction of cut when using a router, and that it is the most important aspect of routing. The standard instruction is to cut against the rotation of the cutter, but this can cause confusion. The correct cutting direction can be illustrated with a simple example of a rebate cut with a straight two-flute cutter and the side fence on the router. The steps are as follows:

1. Fit the cutter, decide which way round you are going to hold the router, and fit the side fence on the right.

2. Make the cut by pushing the router away from you along the right-hand side of your workpiece. You will be cutting against the rotation of the cutter. This can be clarified by imagining that the cutter is a tiny high-speed wheel – its direction of rotation is clockwise, looking down on it.

When the router is switched on, the clockwise rotation will make this 'wheel' want to roll back towards you along the edge of the workpiece. By cutting away from you, therefore, you are pushing against the resistance of a cutter that wants to come back to you. At the same time, the clockwise rotation exerts a force on the wood that tries to move the router to your left as it makes the cut. That is why the fence is fitted to the

▲ *Photo 1 Rebate cut halfway along block, showing direction of cut ...*
▼ *Photo 2 ... and the same rebate cut being made with the router pulled*

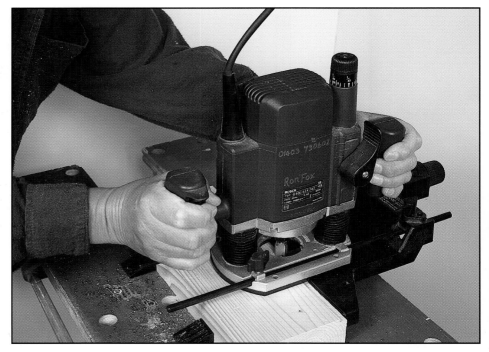

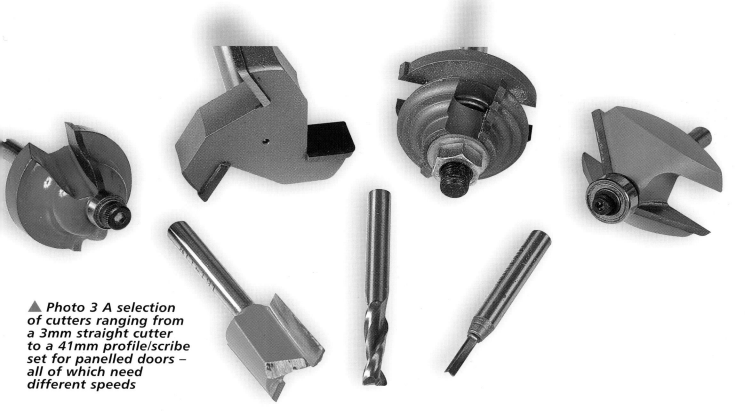

▲ **Photo 3 A selection of cutters ranging from a 3mm straight cutter to a 41mm profile/scribe set for panelled doors – all of which need different speeds**

▼ **Photo 4 Cutter maintenance equipment and cutters stored**

right of the workpiece: the rotational force helps you to hold the fence into the work.

It is the combination of these two factors, pushing against the rotation of a cutter that wants to come back towards you, and having the fence on the side that automatically holds it into the workpiece, that makes this the correct direction of cut for hand-held routing. *Photo 1* shows the rebate cut halfway along the block, showing clearly the direction of cut.

Pushing and pulling

In the above example we made the cut by pushing the router, but there is no reason why the router should not be pulled if this is more convenient. *Photo 2* shows the same rebate cut being made with the router pulled. Note that the router is going in the same direction, relative to the cutter rotation, as before.

The rule is that it does not matter whether the router is pushed or pulled so long as it is going in its correct direction.

Looking again at our block of wood, we can make two generalisations: cut anticlockwise around the outside of a figure, and clockwise around the inside.

"It does not matter whether the router is pushed or pulled so long as it is going in its correct direction"

"A rule of thumb is that if you are producing fluffy chippings and shavings, as opposed to splinters or dust, you are not going far wrong"

◀ *Photo 5 The Bosch 900ACE router fitted with a false wooden fence*

"The larger the diameter of the cutter the faster the peripheral speed for a given rpm"

Rate of feed

The next question to deal with is the rate at which to move the router through the work. Too fast and you overload the motor, and splinter and chip the workpiece. Too slow and you will burn the wood.

So, what is the correct rate of feed? Titman, in one of their publications, give a rate of feed of 6 metres per minute in soft-wood and 5 metres per minute in hardwood. This is faster than most of us are likely to go but it represents an optimum rate, if you can attain it. Within the upper limit, the faster you go the less wear on the cutter. In practice you will move at a speed that is comfortable, but a rule of thumb is that if you are producing fluffy chippings and shavings, as opposed to splinters or dust, you are not going far wrong.

Cutter speed

Many, if not most, of the routers currently available are provided with variable speed. A common error among beginners is to drastically reduce the speed, with the idea of

making the cut easier for themselves. Cutter speed, however, should be determined by the job in hand. There are two main applications of the speed control:

● Cutter diameter – the critical factor with router cutters, as with sawblades, is the peripheral speed. The larger the diameter of the cutter, the faster the peripheral speed for a given rpm. Most cutter suppliers give guidance on cutter speeds; typical recommendations are:

Up to 25mm	24,000 rpm
30–50mm	18,000 rpm
55–65mm	16,000 rpm
75mm & over	12,000 rpm

● Different materials – most of us buy our routers to work with wood or wood-based materials but they can also be used to cut material such as Perspex and aluminium. For these, special cutters are available from the main suppliers, and should be used at reduced router speeds.

Photo 3 shows a selection of cutters needing different speeds. They range from a 3mm straight cutter to a 41mm profile/scribe set for panelled doors.

▶ *Photo 6 A number of routers fitted with various anti-tilt plates*

Poor-quality cuts

Having sorted out the questions of direction of cut, rate of feed, and router speed, the beginner is still often nonplussed by the poor quality of the cut. The most likely cause of this is a badly maintained cutter. Many beginners buy a starter box of budget-priced cutters without acquiring the cleaning equipment and diamond hone to keep them in good condition. A clean cutter is halfway to a sharp cutter, so this should be the first priority. At intervals, determined by how much use they get, the cutting edges should be refreshed with a few strokes of a fine-grade diamond hone. (*See page 9 for care of cutters.*)

A trivial, but common, cause of cutter damage is to keep them loose in a bag or box where they rattle around against other tools. If you buy a boxed set keep the cutters in their box; if you buy individual cutters make a simple drilled block for them. Drill holes of a comfortable clearance size for the shank.

Photo 4 shows cutter maintenance equipment and cutters stored in boxes or in drilled blocks.

"When working on the edge of a panel, for instance moulding a table-top, it is easy to let the router tilt – with disastrous results to the cut"

Two basic problems

With all the above problems sorted out there remain two basic hand-routing problems to dog the beginner – run-in or run-out, and tilt.

Run-in or run-out

With the side fence fitted to the router it is very easy to snag the fence at the beginning of the cut. This is the run-in problem. As the cut is completed the leading end of the fence runs off the workpiece and the rotational force of the cutter tries to throw the router to the left, spoiling the end of the cut – the run-out problem.

A simple solution is to fit a false wooden fence to the router side fence. *Photo 5* shows such a fence fitted to the Bosch 900 ACE router. The unbroken length of the false fence allows the cut to be entered and exited, finished cleanly. A very convenient source of hardwood strip for false fences is

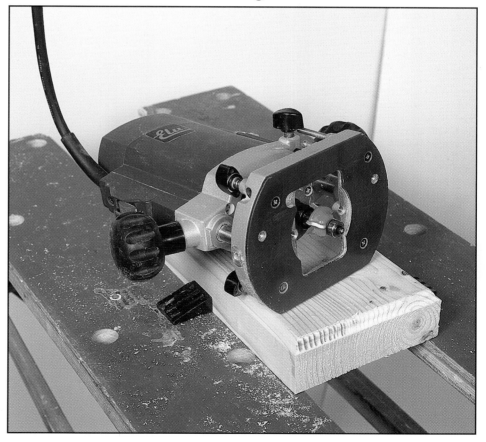

▲ *Photo 7 Method of using a simple home-made plate*
▼ *Photo 8 Softwood with burnt end grain*

▲ *Photo 9 End grain of a shelf with the reverse cut completed*

"The judicious use of reverse cuts is one of the most useful of routing techniques"

the ready-made lipping available from timber merchants and DIY stores. I recently bought a 2m length of 10 × 20mm (⅜ × ¾in) strip for about £2.

Tilt
When working on the edge of a panel, for instance moulding a table top, it is easy to let the router tilt – with disastrous results to the cut. There are various ways of overcoming this problem, but one of the simplest, and most effective, is to make an anti-tilt plate to fit to the base of the router. The plate is fitted with a handle and the router is used with the plate pressed to the surface of the work to prevent the router tilting.

Photo 6 shows a number of routers fitted with various forms of anti-tilt plate. For large, heavy routers the type of plate shown, attached to the Hitachi M12V, is more suitable than the pear-drop shape fitted to the Elu 96E and the Festo OF900E. This large plate can be fitted with two handles and the router propelled around the workpiece without the hands actually being on the router.

For those with a router table, the insert plate used to suspend the router from the table offers a ready-made anti-tilt plate, provided it can be removed and replaced without much trouble. In *Photo 6* the Elu 97E is shown fitted with the insert plate from the Trend Craftsman router table.

Photo 7 demonstrates the method of using the simple home-made plate. The Festo OF900E is being used to put a moulding around the edge of a block of softwood.

Reverse direction
Finally we consider a group of common problems that are all solved by cutting in the reverse direction. Having said earlier that there is a right and wrong direction of cut this seems to be a contradiction. In fact, the judicious use of reverse cuts is one of the most useful of routing techniques. Three particular conditions apply to their use:
● The cut is always made for a specific purpose, for instance, to remove burn marks.

● The cut is nearly always a light one.
● As it is done deliberately, you are aware that you are cutting in the wrong direction, and are therefore on your guard against possible errors.

Burning the wood
Many beginners burn the wood, especially when working on end grain. A number of possible reasons contribute to this – blunt cutters, or too deep a cut leading to too slow a cut. Prevention is better than cure, and practice will overcome most of the problems, but there will still be occasions when the end grain gets scorched, especially with softwood.

The solution is to make a reverse cut without altering the depth of cut. The router is positioned on the far side of the cut, switched on, and pulled lightly and smoothly back across the workpiece. The cut meets our three criteria above: the purpose is to remove the burn; the cut is light – theoretically you are removing no wood at all – and you are doing it knowingly.

The technique is not 100% guaranteed but in most cases it completely removes the burn.

Photo 8 shows a block of softwood with burnt end grain. Half of the burn has been removed by reverse cutting.

Breakout
Breakout is one of the main problems in routing. It invariably occurs on end grain as the cutter exits the workpiece – because the cutter blades are cutting at right angles to the grain of the wood. There are a number of solutions to the problem. The classic one is to clamp or pin a piece of scrap wood on the exit side of the cut so that the breakout occurs as the cutter exits the scrap rather than the workpiece.

An alternative technique is to begin each pass by making a short reverse cut, from the exit side of the cut, back towards the middle. This is akin to hand-planing end grain where you plane both sides towards the middle. After each back pass is made, the router is brought to the beginning of the cut, and the pass made in the normal direction.

A similar technique can be applied when cutting through housings.

Photo 9 shows the end grain of a shelf with the reverse cut completed.

Rippled edge mouldings
Minor wobbles of the router, when moulding the edge of a panel, can leave tiny ripples in the edge. These ripples are often almost invisible to the eye, but they will certainly become visible when the panel is polished. It pays, therefore, to 'inspect' the moulded edges with the fingertips, which will detect any minor irregularities. If any are found they can be removed by pulling a careful reverse cut along the affected edge.

"These ripples are often almost invisible to the eye, but they will certainly become visible when the panel is polished"

Clear cut

Photo 1 *Selection of workpieces with 'wrong' direction cuts, and a dovetail jig that utilises this type of cut for a clean joint*

Clearing up confusion over cutting direction

ONE of the first things the newcomer to routing has to grasp is that there is a right and wrong direction of cut. I covered the basics *on pages 22-3*, but it's good to recap.

The cutter rotates in a clockwise direction as you look down on it and the cut is made against this rotation. As you push the router, the force of the rotation makes the cutter want to come back towards you and move to its left, taking the router with it.

If the router side fence is fitted on the right-hand side of the cut, the clockwise rotational force will keep the fence pulled into the cut. It is the combination of these

two factors that makes this the correct direction of cut. You are pushing against the resistance of a cutter that wants to come back towards you, and the cutter works with you in holding the fence against the workpiece.

'Wrong way'
If you try to cut with the rotation, the cutter will want to run away from you. The force of the rotation will still want to move the router to its left, but this now takes it away from the workpiece.

Cutting a wrong-way cut is harder to control because you have to do the work of

restraining the cut and holding the fence into the workpiece.

The correct direction is when the router is being pushed and the fence is situated on the right-hand edge of the workpiece (*see photo 2*). The cut in the photo happens to involve the router side fence, but the same considerations would apply if the router was guided by a straightedge clamped to the work, or by a bearing-guided moulding cutter.

In all cases the cut is made on the right-hand edge of the workpiece with the straightedge, or bearing, preventing the router moving to its left.

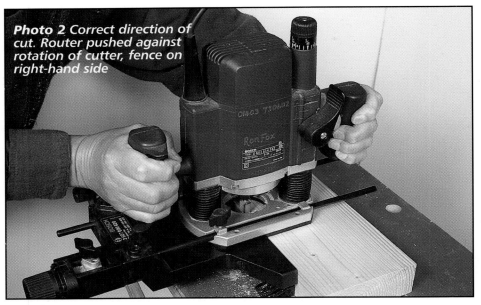

Photo 2 *Correct direction of cut. Router pushed against rotation of cutter, fence on right-hand side*

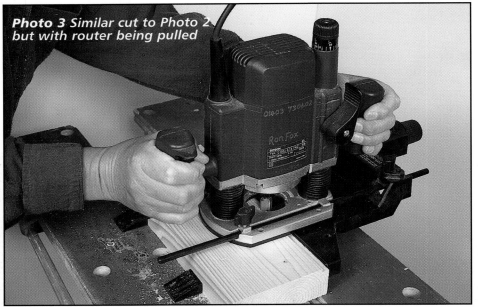

Photo 3 *Similar cut to Photo 2 but with router being pulled*

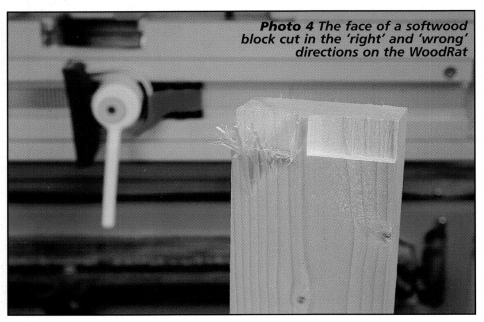

Photo 4 *The face of a softwood block cut in the 'right' and 'wrong' directions on the WoodRat*

It doesn't matter if you push or pull the router as long as it moves in the direction that it wants to go. Many workers prefer to cut a rebate by pulling the router towards them (*see photo 3*). From the operator's position the cutter and the fence appear to be on the left-hand side of the workpiece, but from the router's point of view the cut is the same as in *photo 2*.

This is the basic rule of routing, and inadvertent cutting in the wrong direction brings more grief to the beginner than any other aspect of routing, so be aware of which way you are cutting.

> ## "Inadvertent cutting in the wrong direction brings more grief to the beginner than any other aspect of routing"

Cleaner cuts

What if we deliberately make a cut in the wrong direction? A light cut is much easier to control because less material is removed, so there is less interaction between the cutter and the workpiece.

We will get a cleaner cut, with far less breakout, by going in the 'wrong' direction. If we had power-feed we would make most cuts with the rotation. This is how metal milling is done – the workpiece goes with the rotation, but is secured firmly and power fed.

The softwood block was cut in a WoodRat (*see photo 4*) with half the width against the rotation and half with the rotation.

The difference is self evident. It is possible because, in the WoodRat the router can be clamped firmly in position, the workpiece clamped securely in the cutting position, and the cut made by wheeling the wood past the cutter with the hand crank. Although not strictly power feed, this system has the same effect.

Cutting in the wrong direction goes under various other names such as 'climb-cutting' and 'down-cutting'. With the latter, the opposite is, quite logically, 'up-cutting'.

A clean-edged rebate

When dealing with difficult grain, we can get a clean edge on a rebate by making a preliminary reverse cut (*see photo 5*) at full depth but very little width. Because the cut removes very little wood it is controllable even though it is in the wrong direction.

After the initial reverse cut, the side fence is set to the full width of the rebate and the cut proceeds in the normal way.

Photo 5 To produce a rebate with a clean edge on timber with difficult grain, first reverse cut at full depth but with very little width

Moulding end grain

An ever-present problem with routing is end grain breakout. For this reason we usually make end grain cuts first, so the long-grain cuts can clean away the breakout.

Sometimes a job involves routing end grain without following on round the long grain, such as moulding the two ends and front of a shelf. For a batch of shelves tack a breakout piece behind the workpiece.

Alternatively, we can make an initial reverse cut on the output side of the end grain and then make the remainder of the cut in the correct direction (*see photo 6*). This is the same idea as hand planing end grain by working from both sides towards the middle.

Removing end grain burn

If you are ever going to burn a cut it is likely to be on softwood end grain. This can be repaired by taking a slightly deeper cut to remove the burnt material, but there is a limit to this process if it doesn't work first time.

A method that frequently succeeds, although not fully guaranteed, is to make a reverse cut (*see photo 7*) without altering the depth of cut. The reverse cut should be a smooth skimming cut which, since the depth of cut has not been changed, removes no material – at least in theory.

Preventing breakout

The classic method for preventing breakout on boards and housings is to clamp a scrap piece of the same material where the cut emerges, but an alternative is to begin each cut by nicking back into the board on the output side (*see photo 8*).

This is a simple operation for through housings and, of course, does not arise with stopped housings.

Finishing moulded edges

Having moulded the edges of a panel, such as for a table top, run your fingertips along each edge before you remove the cutter from your router.

Even if you have used an anti-tilt plate your fingers might detect tiny ripples and bumps which are not visible to the naked

Photo 6 The end grain of a shelf is reverse cut to prevent breakout

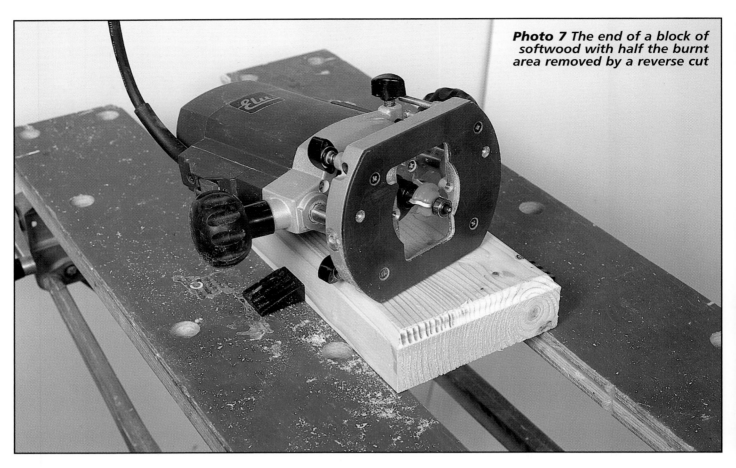

eye. They will certainly become visible when you polish the panel though.

Remove them by going round again at full depth of cut, in the wrong direction, with smooth skimming cuts.

Trimming laminates and lippings

When applying plastic laminate to the horizontal and vertical surfaces of a panel, the vertical laminate is trimmed flush before the horizontal laminate is applied.

Similarly, hardwood lipping applied to the edge of a bench top usually needs to be trimmed flush. If you use the bottom of a straight cutter for this job the trimming has to be done with a reverse cut so as not to knock the laminate away

"Follow the rule, clockwise around the inside of a figure"

from the edge of the workpiece.

Cutting in the wrong direction produces a 'hammer and anvil' effect and avoids breaking the glue joint. This, in fact, is one case where the 'wrong-way' cut is the only 'right' cut.

Formica lipping is trimmed, using a home-made 'step' board to position a straight cutter immediately over the lip (*see photo 9*). A fine height adjuster on the router helps set the cut so that the laminate ends up exactly flush with the surface of the panel.

Trammel bar

When cutting a circle in a board, the correct direction of cut depends on whether you are cutting the disc, such as for a breadboard, or whether you are cutting the hole, such as for a loudspeaker cabinet.

If you are making a breadboard, or a circular table top, you should cut anti-clockwise following the basic rule of 'anti-clockwise around the outside of a figure'.

If you are cutting a hole for the front of a loudspeaker cabinet or a clock face, the

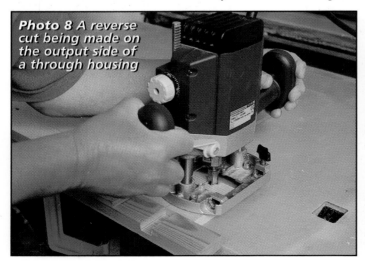

Photo 8 *A reverse cut being made on the output side of a through housing*

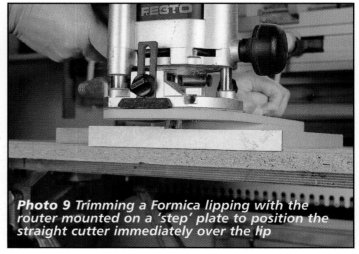

Photo 9 *Trimming a Formica lipping with the router mounted on a 'step' plate to position the straight cutter immediately over the lip*

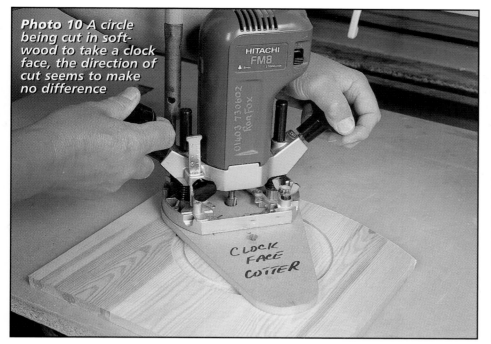

Photo 10 A circle being cut in softwood to take a clock face, the direction of cut seems to make no difference

"Try various cuts in the wrong direction to see what you can get away with"

Dovetailing

Reverse cutting is commonplace in dovetailing. With the simpler jigs, where the pins and tails are cut simultaneously, the initial cut is a reverse cut from right to left across the tailboard to give a crisp clean inside edge to the board (*see photo 11*).

With more sophisticated jigs such as the Leigh, reverse cutting is used to give the same crisp clean edges to the pins of through dovetails.

It is important to remember we are making the cut for a specific purpose. When you have gained some routing experience, it is instructive to try various cuts in the wrong direction to see what you can get away with.

Begin with extremely light cuts and increase gradually until the cut gets difficult to control. If the cut is manageable you will get a cleaner result.

hole is your end product, in which case you follow the rule 'clockwise around the inside of a figure'.

In practice you are likely to have trouble whatever you do, because there will be tearout at the two points on the circle where the cutter is going at right angles to the grain.

The best results come from approaching these two points from both directions. This does not apply to materials such as MDF.

The theoretical direction of cut is clockwise, but there was no discernible difference between clockwise and anti-clockwise in this case (*see photo 10*).

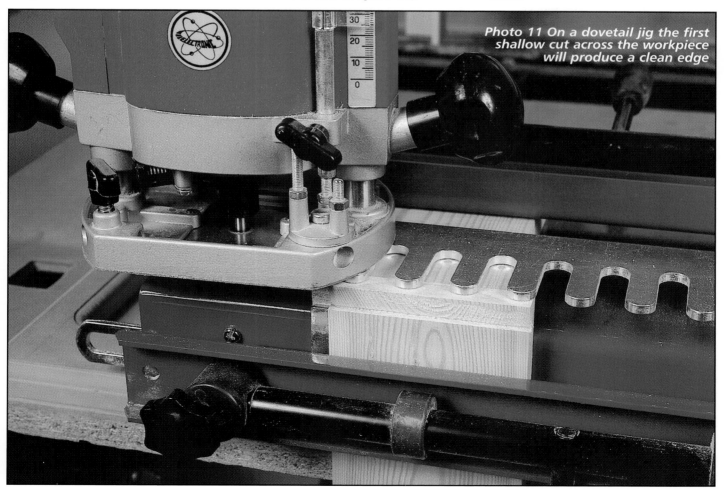

Photo 11 On a dovetail jig the first shallow cut across the workpiece will produce a clean edge

Holding the
workpiece

▲ *Photo 1 Various holding devices*

WITH routing projects, perhaps even more so than with other areas of woodwork, holding the work is often the most difficult part of the job. A rule of thumb is that the larger the workpiece the more likely you are to clamp it to the bench, or to trestles, and take the router to the work; conversely the smaller the workpiece the more convenient it is to use the router in a router table and move the workpiece past the cutter. This article illustrates some of the readily available ways of holding the work when hand routing. With table work, holding devices fall into the category of jigs which will be covered on another occasion.

The Workmate
The Workmate has been justly described as the router user's best friend and tends to be taken for granted. The dual height model is particularly useful since at full height it holds the work directly at a comfortable level, while in its lower position it is a convenient height for most small router tables.

I use the Workmate a great deal to hold a simple home-made sacrificial cutting table of chipboard, with one side faced with hardboard (*see pages 71-6*). This is held in place by means of the Workmate clamping pads, which grip the board through holes cut with the router using a guidebush and simple template. The holes do away with the need for a batten on the board and therefore make it

double-sided with the minimum amount of trouble. This cutting table provides the answer to what to hold the work on; it enables you to clamp, pin, tape, or hot-melt glue your workpiece without worrying about marking or cutting into your bench top.

Weights
The simplest ways are still sometimes the best. The Editor mentioned to me his past exploits in casting lead in the bottom of a bucket to use for holding workpieces by sheer weight. My weights are a shade more sophisticated, being old cast-iron barbell weights, a legacy of my misspent youth. I use these quite a lot, though mainly to weigh down stacks of boards or part-finished components (*see photo 1*).

"The Editor mentioned to me his past exploits in casting lead in the bottom of a bucket to use for holding the workpiece by sheer weight"

Clamps

The range of clamping devices available is quite bewildering. The best known are the Record G-clamps which can exert enormous pressure when required and are pretty well guaranteed to hold anything, but they are being superseded for lighter work by the single-handed clamps based on the mastic gun, such as the Solo. These are the ones I use most, particularly for holding straight edges and simple jigs to the workpiece.

Other excellent single-handed clamps,

with the advantage of soft plastic jaws, are the Jorgensen E-Z HOLD bar clamp and the Quick Grip clamps made by Vise-Grip, both of which are made in the USA but are available in the UK. With this style clamp, pumping the sliding handle or squeezing the pistol grip closes the jaws (*see photos 2 and 3*).

For light work where it is important to not mark the surface, Klemmsia cam clamps are useful. These are lightweight hardwood clamps with cork-faced jaws. They are quick to use, although they

▲ *Photo 2 Use of the Solo; the single-handed clamp is holding the trimming jig to the workpiece and worktable*

"The range of clamping devices available is quite bewildering"

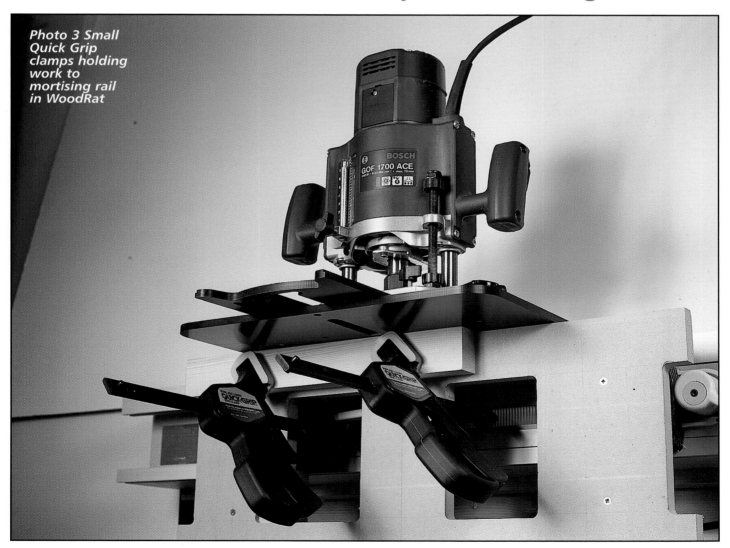

Photo 3 Small Quick Grip clamps holding work to mortising rail in WoodRat

▲ **Photo 4 Large F-clamp holding workpiece for fluting**

require two hands, and the pressure is applied by levering the cam. They are available in lengths up to 1200mm and are much cheaper than corresponding sash cramps, although far less powerful. I use them for clamping boxes, drawers and the like, where the strength of the joint is in the fit and great pressure is not required.

F-clamps are available in sizes ranging from 100mm to well over 1000mm when fully extended. The smaller ones are a menace to tighten unless you drill a hole through the wooden handle for a tommy bar. The larger ones are useful for holding lengths of timber for operations such as fluting a tapered leg. The workpiece is put into the clamps and the bar of the clamp held in the bench vice. If necessary, stabilising blocks can be placed under the workpiece (*see photo 4*).

Handscrews

Handscrews are far more widely used in North America than in Europe. They come in a variety of sizes and are very useful for holding odd shapes, but they take a bit of getting used to. They are handy as improvised vices for small and irregularly shaped work. Mine are Jorgensen and come from Hard to Find Tools, who also trade as Chesterman Marketing.

Toggle clamps

Toggle clamps are used mainly for holding the work in a jig, and are especially useful for batch work where speed and ease of changing the workpiece are important. I also use them to fasten certain router models into a router table, where the router does not have convenient fastening holes in its base plate. You will continually find new uses for them.

"I find double-sided tape useful for so many different purposes, and wonder how we ever managed without it"

Zyliss vice

The Zyliss vice is an expensive but extremely versatile multipurpose vice capable of holding work in numerous different ways and at various angles. It is part of a comprehensive system of workpiece manipulation but performs well on its own (*see photo 5*).

Double-sided tape

I find double-sided tape useful for so many different purposes, and wonder how we ever managed without it. I use a heavy-duty carpet tape, which I obtain from the local DIY superstore. I use it to hold workpieces to the cutting table for guidebush work or when cutting circles and ellipses, for fastening a pattern to the workpiece for batch work on the router table, and for numerous other odd jobs (*see photo 6*). The art of using it is to gauge how little is needed rather than how much; the hardest part of the job is often releasing the workpiece after cutting!

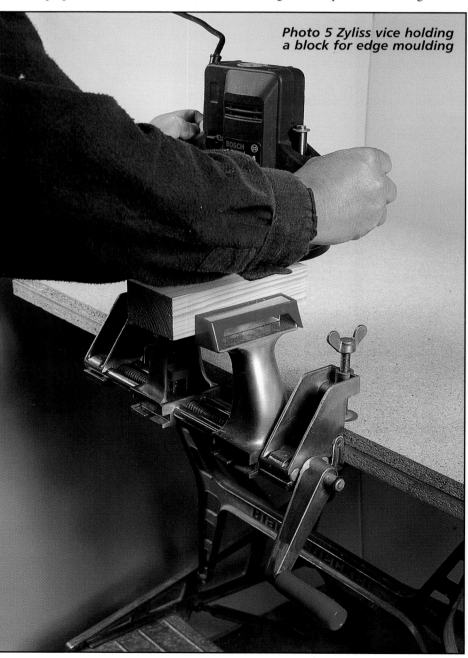

Photo 5 Zyliss vice holding a block for edge moulding

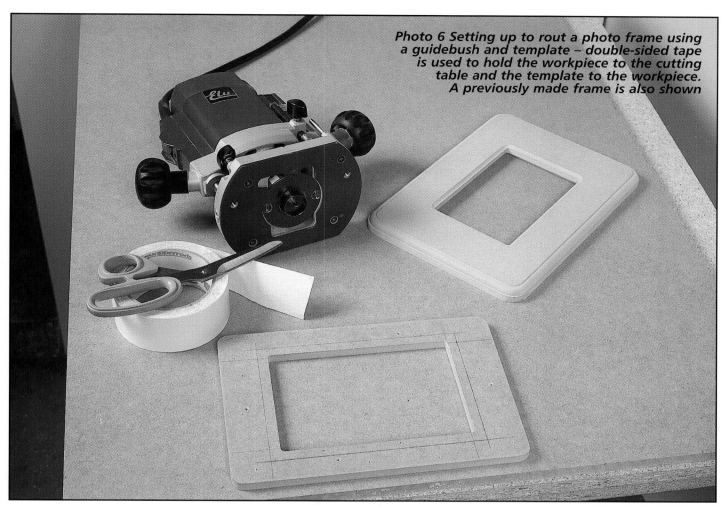

Photo 6 Setting up to rout a photo frame using a guidebush and template – double-sided tape is used to hold the workpiece to the cutting table and the template to the workpiece. A previously made frame is also shown

Hot melt glue gun

The hot melt glue gun is another fairly recent innovation, which performs a number of the functions of double-sided tape. It is not an alternative to ordinary glues but for many odd jobs the gun is almost as good as having an extra pair of hands. It pays to buy an industrial grade gun; the cheap DIY models are so low powered that the glue never reaches its proper operating temperature, consequently the setting time is only about 15 seconds which is far too short a time to position the work. I now use a BEA 220 for which a range of glue sticks with different setting times are available.

A tip for freeing the workpiece is to soften the glue with acetone and the work will lift clear with a minimum of mess. If you use nail-varnish remover make sure it is acetone, as many modern removers are non-acetone.

▶ Photo 7 Freehand routing with the workpiece held on a Mini-Mach vacuum table

"The vacuum table is the ultimate work-holding device with a number of particularly relevant uses for routing"

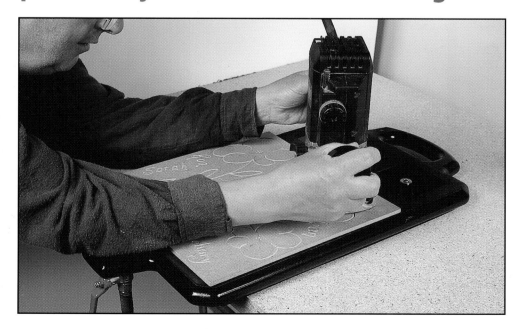

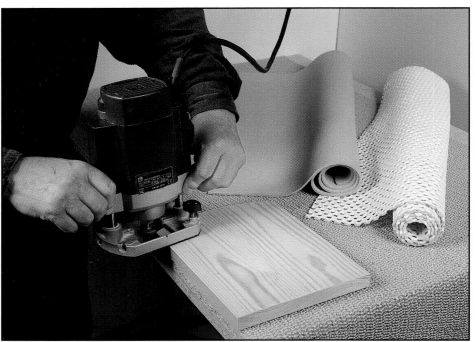

▲ Photo 8 Several different router mats – in the foreground a small panel is being edge moulded

range the Mini-Mach has the same applications as the old V-Mach. It is now exclusively distributed by Trend and has a list price of £75.37 inc VAT.

Router mat

Finally, one of my personal favourites is the router mat. This is simply a sheet of one of the current crop of non-slip materials developed primarily to stop rugs and carpets slipping on hard floors. The mat is spread on the bench top, or in my case the cutting table on my Workmate, the workpiece is laid on the mat and the router taken to it in the usual way. The router mat is particularly suitable for edge moulding and freehand work. While not in the same class as the vacuum table it is not in the same price bracket either. I use two mats: one from Axminster Power Tools sold in a 900 × 600mm (3 × 2ft) piece and one from my local ironmonger called a Rug Stop sold in a 1200 × 600mm (4 × 2ft) roll. A number of alternative versions, under different brand names, are appearing. One of the most recent is the Grip Mat, distributed by Draper and available from their stockists.

As with toggle clamps and the hot melt glue gun, the more you use the router mat the more uses you will find for it (*see photo 8*).

The vacuum table

The vacuum table is the ultimate work-holding device with a number of particularly relevant uses for routing. Firstly it will hold panels, such as table tops, for edge moulding and surface decoration; secondly, it is good for holding template and workpiece profile cutting and guidebush work; thirdly, it will hold panels and practice pieces for freehand routing.

For work that involves cutting right through the workpiece, a lightweight porous grade of MDF can be used as a sacrificial board. This is placed on the vacuum table and the workpiece placed on top. The vacuum holds both boards firmly to the surface of the table, allowing the cut to go through the workpiece into the sacrificial board.

The Mini-Mach vacuum table is now marketed by Trend. The larger V-Mach,

which came complete with built-in vacuum motor, and had to be mounted on a Workmate or a bench is no longer available.

The best-known vacuum table is the Mini-Mach. It requires connection to a domestic vacuum cleaner or workshop dust extractor to provide the vacuum (*see photo 7*). It mounts on a bench top and the vacuum grips the bench as well as the workpiece. Within its more limited

"The art of using it is to gauge how little is needed rather than how much; the hardest part of the job is often releasing the workpiece after cutting!"

Suppliers

■ For a general range of clamps, toggle clamps, hot melt glue guns, and router mat:
Axminster Power Tool Centre, Chard Street, Axminster, Devon, EX13 5DZ
Tel: 01297 33656

■ For Jorgensen handscrews, E-Z HOLD clamps, Klemsia, and other clamping devices:
Hard to Find Tools, 16 Badgers Croft, Eccleshall, Stafford, ST21 6DS
Tel: 01785 250342

■ For Zyliss vice and accessories:
John Mills Ltd, JML House, Regis Road, Kentish Town, London NW5 3EG Tel: 0207 691 3800

■ For Mini-Mach vacuum table, clamps, and double-sided tape:
Trend Machinery and Cutting Tools Ltd, Unit 6, Odhams Trading Estate, Watford, Hertfordshire, WD2 5TR
Tel: 01923 249911

Doctor depth

Examining fine height adjusters

AMONG the many accessories available for the router, fine height adjusters are one of the most useful. In this chapter I will explore the range of fine height adjusters available, and see how fine adjusters can be interchanged between models, or made at home for particular routers.

"Several models lend themselves to home-made fine height adjusters"

▼ *Photo 1 Selection of routers with various fine height adjusters: built-in, commercial and home-made*

▼ *Photo 2 The Freud OF2000 and the Ryobi RE 601 have built-in adjusters*

Fine height adjusters

I consider a fine height adjuster, by which I mean the kind that prevents the router rising from its plunged position, to be an essential item of routing kit.

Apart from its obvious use – the precise setting of depth of cut – it also acts as a safety measure when dovetailing with those jigs which use a guidebush narrower than the bottom of the

dovetail cutter. The consequences of inadvertently releasing the plunge lock and letting the spinning cutter come up through the guidebush are drastic and best avoided.

▼ *Photo 3 The DeWalt DW 621, the Elu 177E with the Trend/Elu adjuster, and the Trend T9 with the FHA002 adjuster. The same adjuster also fits the Metabo OFE 1812 and the Woodcut 1800*

▲ **Photo 4** *The Trend T5 fitted with their FHA001 fine height adjuster and DW613 fitted with Elu 96 fine height adjuster, plus some of the other routers that also take the same adjuster*

The fine height adjuster also makes depth of cut setting relatively easy when the router is inverted in a table, although the WoodRat PlungeBars are even better.

For table use, a further option for certain routers, including the DeWalt 625, Hitachi M12V, Makita 3612C and Ryobi RE 601, is the Veritas Router Jack.

Router manufacturers are not consistent in the provision of fine height adjusters. Some models, such as the Bosch GOF 900 and GOF 1300, the Freud FT 2000 and the Ryobi RE 601, have built-in adjusters.

Others such as the DeWalt and Trend ranges offer adjusters as an accessory. Others still, such as Hitachi, Makita and Festo, either use simplified systems based on nuts or rings on a threaded rod, or make no provision at all.

Photo 2 shows two large routers with built-in fine height adjusters, the Freud OF2000 and the Ryobi RE 601. *Photo 3* shows a number of routers fitted with manufacturer's accessory adjusters. The DW621 adjuster could usefully be made 12–15mm longer to give easier handling.

Fortunately, there is a certain amount of interchangeability among models, and when this fails, it is possible to make simple but efficient adjusters for some models.

Interchangeability of commercial adjusters

Photo 4 shows the Trend T5 fitted with the FHA 001 adjuster and the DeWalt DW613 router fitted with my Elu 96E adjuster, plus some of the other routers that will also take them.

"Fortunately, there is a certain amount of interchangeability among models"

✦ **Photo 5** *From left to right: the Trend T5 and Elu 96 adjusters, together with the DeWalt adjuster for the DW 621 and the Trend adjusters for the Elu 177/DW 625 and T9. Note the additional length of the Trend T5 adjuster compared with the old Elu 96 one*

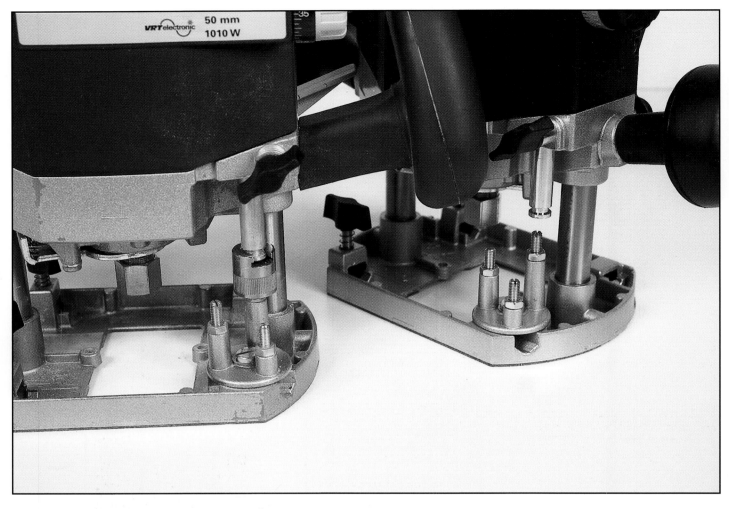

These adjusters are available as accessories and screw on to the longest of the 5mm threaded rods in the base turret. They are operated by screwing up or down to set the depth of plunge.

This kind of fine height adjuster locks the router in position, such that if the plunge lock is released it can be neither lowered nor raised. This is not the case with the built-in adjusters on the Freud and Ryobi, or with the adjuster supplied by DeWalt for the DW 625.

The Trend T5 adjuster is very similar to the old Elu 96 one, but is a bit longer because the T5 is slightly taller than the MOF 96. This means the Trend adjuster can be used on the Elu but not vice-versa. A similar kind of adjuster is available for the Elu 97/ DeWalt DW 621, but this does not fit any other router as far as I know.

The Trend FHA 001 and Elu 96 adjusters can also be used on several other models including the DeWalt 613, the Perles OF808, the Einhell EOF 850, and the Power Devil PDW 850.

The Perles OF808E must have the T5 adjuster because of the extra height of the motor housing to accommodate the variable-speed board; the others will take either. The Trend T9 adjuster also fits the Metabo OFE 1812 and the Woodcut 1800.

Photo 5 shows the Trend T5 and Elu 96 adjusters together with the DeWalt adjuster for the DW 621 and the Trend

▲ ***Photo 6** Close-up of the HolzHer 2356 fitted with its fine height adjuster. This adjuster also fits the Atlas Copco OFSE 1000, also shown*

▼ ***Photo 7** Three box spanners with appropriate nuts hammered into their ends to make fine adjusters*

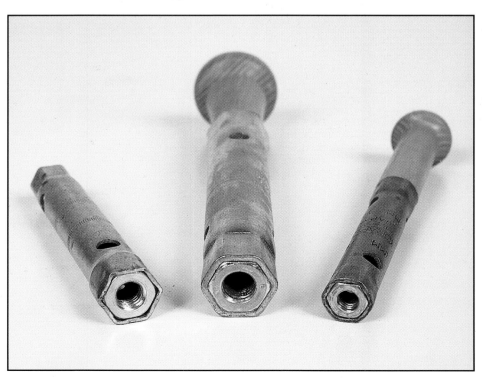

"You can finish it off with a handle made from a piece of dowel or broomstick"

adjusters for the Elu 177/ DW 625 and Trend T9. Here you can see the additional length of the Trend T5 adjuster compared with the one on the old Elu 96.

HolzHer adopt a different approach with their 2356 model. A threaded link is screwed to one of the turret rods and the top is clipped to the bottom of the stop bar. Height is set by releasing the plunge-lock lever and rotating the depth-setting wheel.

As with the Trend T5 and DeWalt 621 systems, the HolzHer fine height adjuster prevents the router moving either up or down. The HolzHer adjuster also fits the Atlas Copco OFSE 1000.

Photo 6 shows the HolzHer 2356 fitted with its fine height adjuster and the very similar Atlas Copco OFSE 1000.

Home-made adjusters

Several models lend themselves to home-made fine height adjusters. The Hitachi range is a good example. The diameter of the threaded rod on most Hitachis – including the ZK 2008, M8V and M12V – is 8mm, which means that the nuts require a 13mm spanner.

All you have to do is to hammer an 8mm nut, preferably the self-locking type with a nylon ring in the top, into the end of a 12mm box spanner. Since the 8mm nut normally requires a 13mm spanner, hammering it into a 12mm box spanner causes the spanner to stretch slightly to accept the oversize nut, gripping it tightly without the need for welding, glue, pins etc.

You can finish it off with a handle made from a piece of dowel or broomstick, or you can turn a superior version (*see photo 8*).

At first the adjuster will be stiff to turn as the thread cuts its way into the nylon locking ring, but it will soon ease without working loose. I have been using mine for about five years and it works very well.

Exactly the same kind of adjuster can be made for the Elu 177/DeWalt 625 and the Makita 3612C. For the DeWalt 625, the studding is 13mm, which gives a nut with 19mm spanner flats which is hammered into the end of an 18mm box spanner.

For the Makita the studding is 10mm, which has 17mm spanner flats, and so is hammered into the end of a 16mm box spanner. Photo 7 shows three box spanners with appropriate nuts hammered into their ends, and a selection of home-made adjusters fitted to various routers can be seen in *photo 8*.

The principle is the same in all cases. The adjuster is based on a length of studding with a nut in the end of a box spanner.

With the small size of nut required for the small routers, it is very difficult to hammer them into a box spanner 1mm smaller, so, for anything less than 8mm studding, I use epoxy resin glue to set the nut into the spanner.

▼ *Photo 8 A selection of home-made adjusters. Hitachi M8V, DeWalt DW 625, Makita 3612C, Bosch 400 and Festo OF 900*

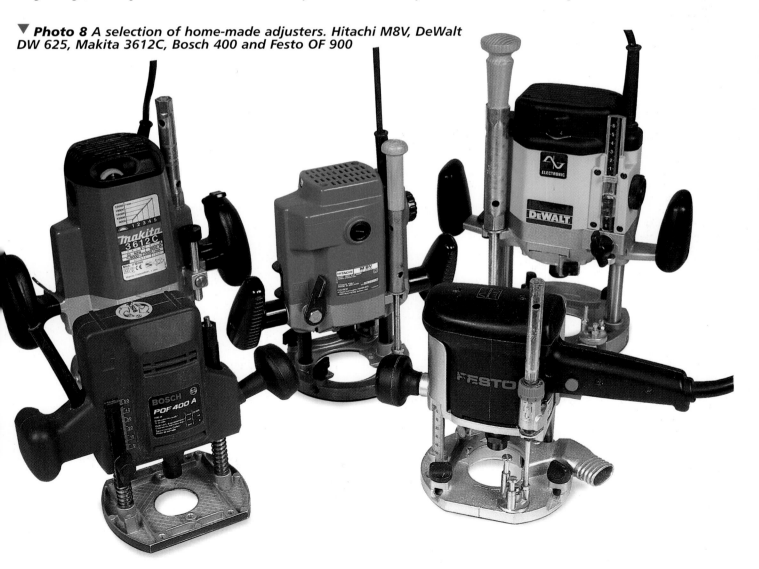

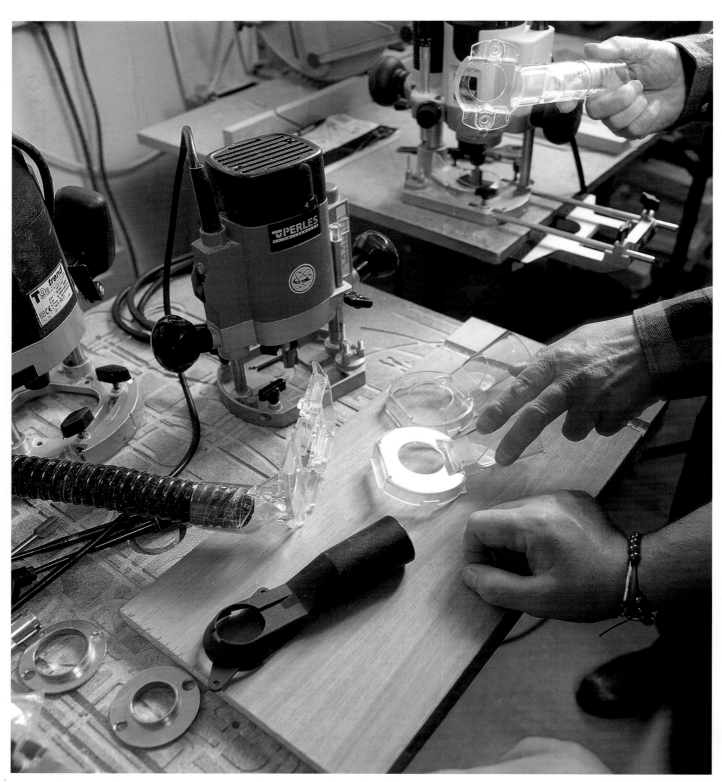

Comparing different dust extractor spouts

Under the table

The benefits of using a router table

THE biggest single step beginners can take in expanding the scope of their routing is to buy or build a router table. A general rule of routing is that the larger the workpiece the better it is to clamp the work and move the router, while the smaller the workpiece the better it is to anchor the router and move the work.

The router table is the most common method of anchoring the router, leaving the hands free to hold the workpiece and move it past the cutter. Table routing has a number of potential advantages over hand-held routing:
a) It is much less stressful, with far less crouching, squinting and gripping;
b) Small workpieces can be routed more accurately and, with the appropriate guards, safely;
c) The scope is wider. Many large diameter cutters are manufactured for use only in tables or overhead routers. You will, however, need a heavy-duty router with $\frac{1}{2}$in collet and variable speed to be able to take full advantage of this;

> "An important aspect of a router table is the size of the hole through which the cutter rises"

▼ *Photo 1 Big Woodcut table with Hitachi M8V fitted with home-made height adjuster and Elu 177E fitted with WoodRat PlungeBar*

d) Dust extraction is much easier to arrange, usually more efficient, and does not get in the way as it can with hand routing;

e) The results are often better than with hand-held routing because it is usually impossible to tilt the workpiece against the cutter;

f) The cutting system is 'fail-safe' because with most cuts it is impossible to over-cut; if the work comes away from the fence or up from the cutter you simply make another pass.

The only drawbacks – which are totally outweighed by the advantages – are:

(i) It can be difficult to change cutters with the router in the inverted position;

(ii) Depth of cut is more awkward to set – a fine height adjuster greatly helps;

(iii) Dust and shavings tend to fall into the router. (Frequent use of a vacuum cleaner remedies this one.)

Commercial tables

Tables can be had from around £70 to more than £1000. Examples include the ISD tables marketed by Charnwood and The Woodcut Trading Company, the Trend 'Craftsman' and Bosch RT60 , the Festo 'Basis Plus', the Record RPR60T, the Titman, the Veritas, and the Trend 'Routerack'.

Of the above, the smallest ISD is the cheapest and is capable of quite serious routing. The Trend is an improved version of a table originally produced by Sears in the USA. The Mk I version is also marketed by Bosch. The largest Charnwood and the Titman offer over-and-under routing.

The Record resembles a small spindle moulder and the Routerack is very expensive for what it is. The Veritas has a

▼ **Photo 2 Sash bar moulding – Little Charnwood W002 table with Elu 96E in it, guards and dust extraction fitted**

patented clamping system to hold the router – of particular interest to owners of the Festo OF9OOE, which has the reputation of being difficult to fit into any table apart from the very expensive Festo 'Basis Plus'.

An important aspect of a router table is the size of the hole through which the cutter rises. It is no good having a strong table which will take a heavy-duty router, then being unable to use the large cutters because they are too big to pass through the hole. A valuable feature, therefore, especially for heavy-duty routers, is a large aperture with a set of reducing rings to allow the hole to be adjusted to suit the cutter being used. Unfortunately, this feature is not always found on otherwise good tables.

I would look first at those from The Woodcut Trading Company.

Home-made tables

One should certainly examine the available proprietary devices – including the provision of guards etc. – before embarking on making one's own. Nevertheless, I firmly believe that the best router table is the one that you make yourself, to your own requirements.

If you decide to make your own, it is possible to buy commercial table inserts, e.g. for the Trend 'Craftsman' and Bosch RT60, or a universal one from The Woodcut Trading Company, from which to hang your router.

The Woodcut version has removable plastic rings to accommodate different cutter diameters and a pivot pin which is used to lead in to cuts made with a bearing-guided cutter in the table.

You can of course make your own insert plate or hang the router directly from a recess in the underside of the table.

"My advice is to make the base first so that the top can be mounted as soon as it is finished"

The fundamental part of a routing table is the top and its provision for hanging the router underneath. The usual material for the top is MDF covered on both surfaces with plastic laminate.

Once made, the top can be: clamped to a Workmate or trestles; bolted or clamped overhanging your bench top; or mounted on a stand, perhaps incorporating cutter storage or dust extractor chute.

Against standard advice, however, I go for making the base first, so that the top can be mounted as soon as it is finished.

"A good big'un will always beat a good little'un"

▲ *Photo 3 Cutting tenon – Trend table with 96E in it. Tenon push block, spiral cutter*

◄ *Photo 4 Scribing door frame – Trend table. Wealden 8mm cutters*

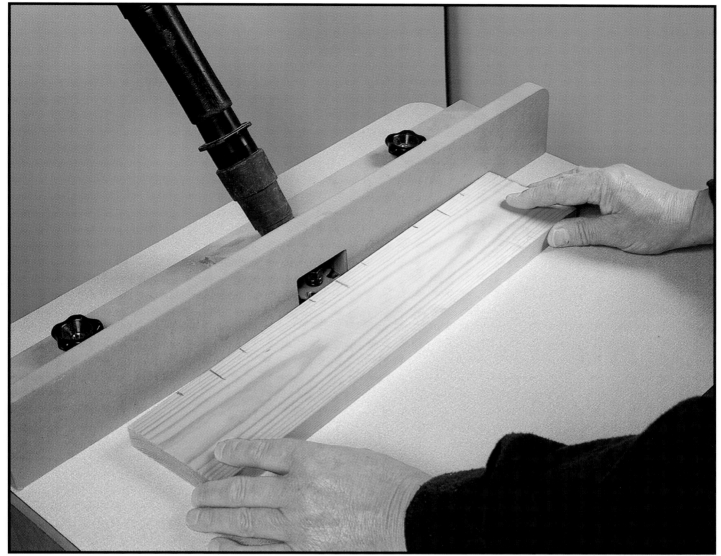

▲ Photo 5 Biscuit jointing –
home-made Festo table. CMT ¼in
arbor biscuit cutter, depth of cut
set with home-made gauge

Routers for router tables

We can take note of the old boxing adage:
a good big'un will always beat a good
little'un. This applies to the router and to
the table it is put in. A router usually works
much harder in a table simply because the
operator doesn't have to work so hard.

It is far less stressful standing at a table
and running lengths of moulding than it is
to hand-rout. Consequently the router
tends to be run continuously for long
periods. In addition, setting the cutter
depth is often such a pantomime that
most users succumb to the temptation to
set the cutter at the full depth of cut and
make one pass only.

This clearly works the router much
harder than taking three light cuts, and
will wear it out quicker than if used
solely hand-held. It is not just a question
of motor power; the bearings and other
components are stressed much more
with a heavy cut.

It is important, therefore, that anyone
contemplating much table work should
consider likely requirements carefully and

choose router and table together.
Unfortunately, for most people it works
the other way round: a router is
purchased and at a later date a table
is bought to go with it.

Virtually any make and model of router
can, however, be fitted to a router table,
but some models are more suitable than
others. The most important requirement is
good depth of plunge because the thickness of the router insert plate reduces the
effective depth of cut.

Routers with particularly good depth of
plunge include the Elu 96, the AEG
OF850SE, the HolzHer 2356 and, most
unusually for a large router, the Bosch
GOF1700 ACE. Those with poor plunge
include the Bosch GOF900ACE and
GOF1300 ACE and the Hitachis, but the
position can be improved by removing the
plastic sole plate before installing the
router in the table.

A different approach to the problem is to
choose a table with as thin an insert plate
as possible. The thinnest are found with the
Trend and Bosch tables and the Veritas.

The two next most useful features
of a router intended for use in a table
are a simple switch and a fine height
adjuster with which to set the depth of
cut. A simple switch is a great asset; fancy
switches, like the 'dead man's
handle' type on the larger Bosch models,
need to be clipped or taped 'ON' and
the router operated from a separate,
preferably NVR, switch on the table.
A fine height adjuster is equally useful;
without one, setting the depth of cut
can drive you mad.

For most routers, the WoodRat
PlungeBars are strongly recommended.
They enable several light cuts to be
taken almost as easily as with a
hand-held router. However, the
PlungeBar needs a large recess or
insert plate to give clearance for the
bars.

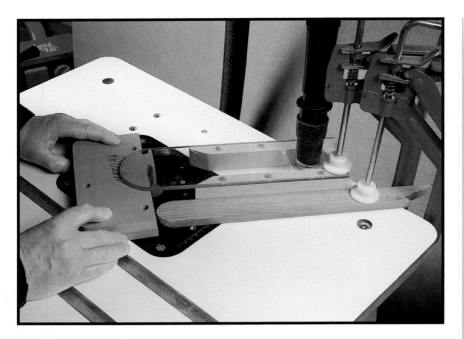

▲ *Photo 6 Pattern moulding – big Woodcut table with home-made guard/dust extraction. Mitre box pattern, ⅜in CMT flush trimmer*

I use the Elu 177E with the PlungeBar, mounted on the Woodcut Trading Company table insert. Drilled and tapped holes in the router baseplate for fastening it to the insert plate are a great advantage, otherwise the guidebush holes have to be used, which can cause the table insert to flex.

If you are planning to use an insert like the Woodcut one, which has a large cutter aperture, check that your router fixing points are wide enough apart to fasten to the plate itself.

The Festo OF900E has no convenient mounting holes in its base, but it fits beautifully in the Veritas table, and a very successful home-made one can be made for it using toggle clamps to hold the router in the table recess.

So consider all the attributes of different routers, and the uses to which you might put them, before buying.

Photo 1 shows two routers suitable for table use: The Hitachi M8V fitted with a home-made fine height adjuster and the Elu 177E fitted with the WoodRat PlungeBar.

▼ *Photo 7 Panel-raising – big home-made table with Elu 177E and PlungeBar. Bearing-guided cutter and home-made guard/extractor. Arched panel, Titman horizontal cutter*

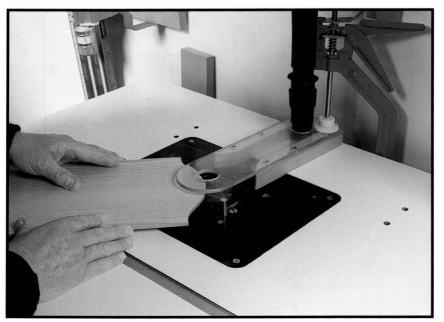

Router Table Work

The information in this panel is devoted to examples of router table work using various router/table combinations.

Sash bar moulding
Photo 2 shows a length of sash bar being moulded on the little Charnwood W002 table fitted with the Elu 96E. The table comes with all the guards, featherboard and dust extractor spout shown in the picture. **Note:** More recent models have a mitre fence slot.

Cutting a tenon
Photo 3 illustrates the cutting of a tenon in the Trend table, using the tenon push block with a scrap piece behind it to prevent break-out. Cutting the tenon vertically uses the length of the cutter blade rather than the bottom and gives a cleaner cut. The cutter being used is a CMT solid carbide upcut spiral. Exactly the same cut can be made in the Bosch table.

Scribing a door frame rail
Photo 4 shows the top rail of a panelled door being scribed on the Trend table using a Wealden reversible door set on an 8mm shank. Note use of mitre fence and scrap piece to prevent breakout.

Biscuit jointing
Photo 5 shows biscuit slots being cut on a home-made table made specifically for the Festo OF 900E router. A CMT 4mm slotting cutter on a ¼in shank is being used with depth of cut controlled by the fence, set with a home-made depth of cut gauge.

Pattern moulding
Photo 6 illustrates the use of a flush trimming cutter with a pattern taped to the workpiece. The job in hand is the cutting of a cheek for the Woodrat mitre box using a CMT ⅜in flush trimming cutter. Note home-made guard/dust extraction and lead-in piece clamped to table.

Panel raising
Photo 7 shows a small panel for an arched door being raised on large home-made router table fitted with the Elu 177E and PlungeBar using a Titman bearing-guided panel-raising cutter. Note home-made guard/dust extraction port and lead-in pin.

Selection of routers with various types of dust-extractor spout fitted

In pursuit of clean living

A serious look at the importance of dust extraction and how to achieve it

DUST is inextricably linked with routing. Its control is one of the major preoccupations of the day, principally because of a growing awareness of the hazards associated with dust, but also because of the wider use of dust-producing materials such as MDF.

In this chapter we look at methods of dust extraction open to the home user, including ambient air filtration.

"A few extractors incorporate a time delay in the socket, allowing the extractor to run on for a short time after the router is switched off"

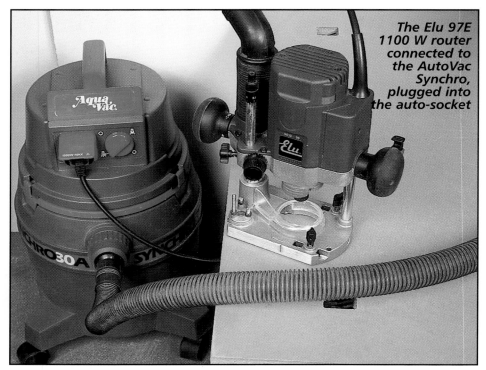

The Elu 97E 1100 W router connected to the AutoVac Synchro, plugged into the auto-socket

"Many people are content with a superannuated domestic model"

Dust extractors

Today's wide range of relatively inexpensive extractors are close relations to the domestic vacuum cleaner, and many people are content with a superannuated domestic model.

More sophisticated workshop versions, however, provide a higher level of protection against dust, with finer filtration and greater capacity containers.

Some models feature automatic switching, whereby the router or other power tool is plugged into a socket on the extractor. Switching the router on or off automatically activates the extractor.

A few extractors incorporate a time delay in the socket, allowing the extractor to run on for a short time after the router is

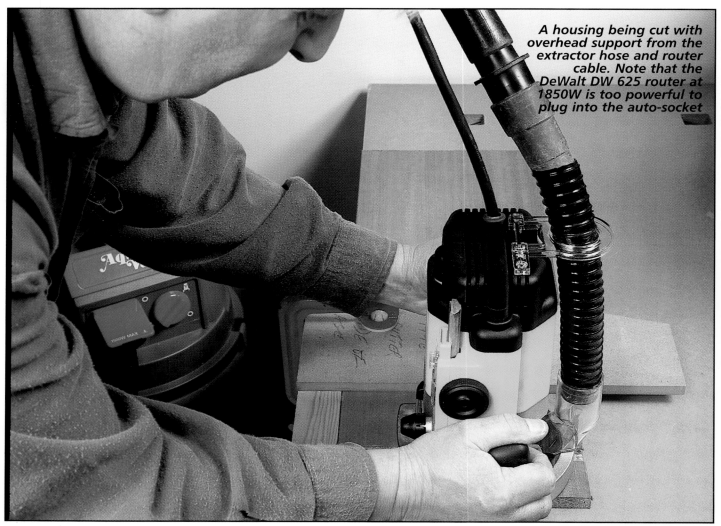

A housing being cut with overhead support from the extractor hose and router cable. Note that the DeWalt DW 625 router at 1850W is too powerful to plug into the auto-socket

switched off. These auto-sockets have a maximum power rating so it is necessary to check whether a particular model will handle, say, your 1800W heavyweight router.

Manufacturers

Makers of suitable extractors include AquaVac, Draper, Numatic and WAP, plus such power tool manufacturers as Bosch, DeWalt, Fein, Festo and Hitachi.

My AquaVac Synchro 30A retails for about £130. It has a paper cartridge renewable filter, a 26-litre container and an auto-socket rated at 1500W.

I cannot use the socket with heavy-duty routers but it is no great hardship to plug and switch the extractor separately (*see photo above left*).

This 'vacuum cleaner' type of extractor is classified as 'HPLV' – 'High Pressure Low Volume' – as distinct from the larger workshop extractors, which are 'HVLP' – 'High Volume Low Pressure'.

Routers, like most portable power tools, require the HPLV type, although I have heard of acceptable results being obtained by stepping down the wider hose of the HVLP type from the usual 100mm (4in) to

"The hoses are invariably of ribbed construction, and have an infuriating knack of snagging on the edge of your bench and holding the router back"

around 50mm (2in).

My Synchro 30A came from one of the DIY Superstores, but is also found in the Screwfix catalogue.

Hand-held routing

Most of today's routers come complete with a dust-extractor spout. Two of the most advanced models, the DeWalt DW621 and the Festo OF 1000EB, incorporate dust extraction in the body of the router.

The DeWalt takes up dust through the main plunge column and the Festo features the extractor duct cast as part of the alloy router base. Both these models extend extraction to the side fence for edge-moulding and similar operations.

Most of the add-on dust extractor spouts stick out, either at the side or the back of the router. This can impede your work, particularly as the hoses are invariably of ribbed construction, and have an infuriating knack

"Tie the extractor hose, fitted with a home-made spout, around your waist at the strategic point – not elegant, but very effective"

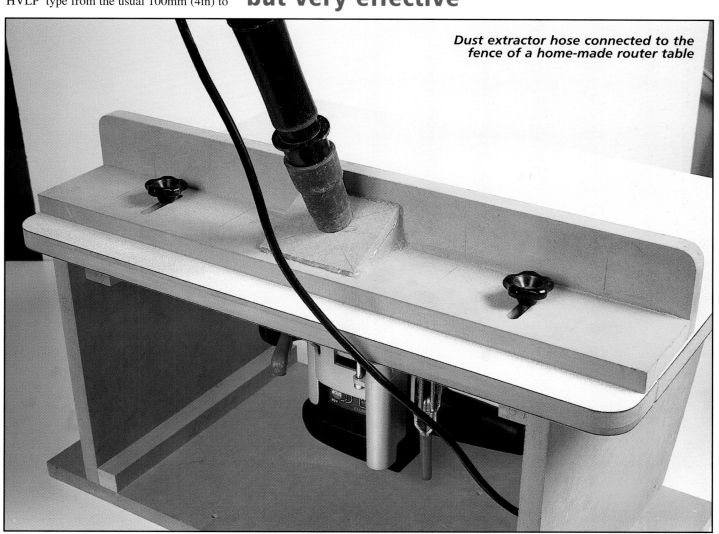

Dust extractor hose connected to the fence of a home-made router table

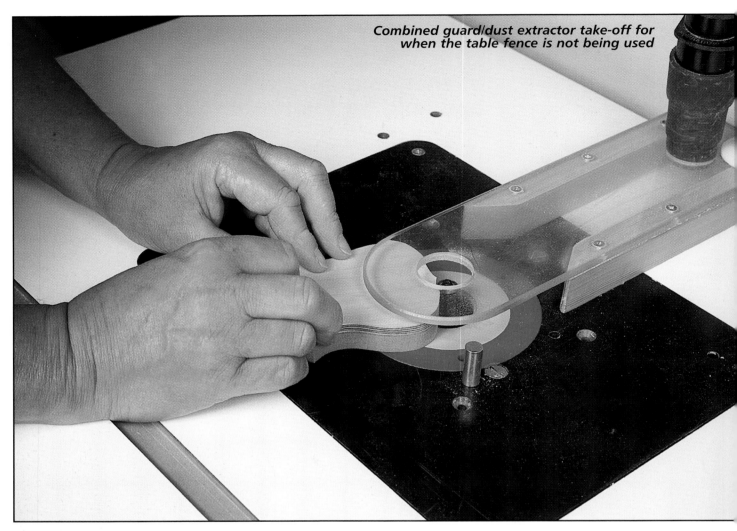

Combined guard/dust extractor take-off for when the table fence is not being used

of snagging on the edge of your bench and holding the router back.

The DeWalt 625 overcomes this problem by allowing the hose to be taken off vertically. Overhead take-off is particularly beneficial if you arrange overhead support for the extractor hose and power cable, and can completely transform your working environment.

It can be arranged for side spouts but it is not as effective as with vertical take-off (*see photo on page 50, bottom*).

Some extractor spouts, notably the Bosch, reduce visibility through the base aperture to practically zero. The current trend seems to be for dust spouts to simply clip on to the router base; others have separate mounting holes and one or two rely on the fence rods to hold the spout in place. The nuisance of fence rods sticking out from the router when the extractor is used without a fence can be overcome by using two short lengths of 8mm silver steel rod, available in 30mm lengths at around £1.50 from good tool shops.

A few, like the Hitachi and the Woodcut, fit by means of the guide bush fixing holes, making the use of dust extraction with guide-bushes awkward.

In practice, however, you might not bother

because most guide bushes act as very effective barriers between the dust and the extractor, and extraction is minimal.

Skeleton form

DeWalt have overcome this problem with the DW 621 by making the guide bushes in skeleton form to allow the passage of dust through them.

The guidebush problem is exacerbated with most dovetailing jigs because the dovetailing comb adds to the obstruction between dust and extractor, and the dust comes flying out from under the comb.

Festo's ingenious fishtail extractor solves this problem for the OF 1000EB, but for non-Festo users I have a more primitive solution. Simply forget the router spout and tie the extractor hose, fitted with a home-made spout – possibly a plastic rainwater duct – around your waist at the strategic point. Not elegant, but very effective.

Unless you are lucky enough to have an extractor fitting which goes straight on the router spout you will need a stepped rubber or plastic bayonet connector to bridge the gap between the two diameters.

Mine is a Draper, but similar fittings are available from Trend.

Table routing

Dust extraction for table routing is an altogether more satisfactory affair because the router and table are static – one hopes – so the hose cannot interfere with your work.

Even though extraction efficiency may be well under 100% it is still well worth using.

The only problem is that some of the dust will inevitably fall into the upturned router, but frequent sucking – not blowing – will minimise the effect of this.

Fence work

The fences on most of today's commercial router tables have provision for connecting an extractor hose, but you will probably have to make or buy a suitable adapter.

With home-made tables, it is a simple matter to make a dust take-off point in the fence.

Cutting a hole in the boxed-in section behind the cutter aperture provides a push fit for your hose (*see photo above*).

Freehand work

Since the dust extraction usually goes with the fence, removing the fence deprives you of the extraction. A simple but effective combined dust extractor/guard can easily be

Permanent cleaner

The Microclene consists of a thin cylindrical sheet-metal drum in which a rotary fan sucks in air through a nylon mesh filter at the bottom of the cylinder. The filter removes particles of dust down to one micron or less.

The filter is hung centrally in the workshop and left running while you work. The MC1000 measures 305 × 230mm (12 × 9in) high, has a 90W motor, filters 1000 cubic metres per hour, and apparently costs some 9p per day to run. Replacement filters are readily available, but my original filter, which I shake out regularly, shows no signs of needing to be replaced.

The filter is changed by unscrewing a central wing nut in the base plate and lowering the plate and filter. A few more millimetres on the threaded rod would make this straightforward job even easier. Another improvement would be an extra metre or so of power cable.

The Microclene range includes both larger and smaller models, the little MC400 being designed specifically for a small workshop of about single-garage size.

The MC1000 has an optional extension tube – a clear plastic 12 or 20in 'skirt' which clips around the bottom of the cylinder, and increases the directional airflow when required; it can be positioned above a specific machine to funnel the airflow, reverting to its normal position, without skirt, for general workshop filtering (see photo).

After working all day in my workshop with the Microclene switched on, my son-in-law remarked that he hadn't had to clean his spectacles once. Highly recommended.

Prices for the Microclene range from about £130.00 for the smallest model to £250.00 for the largest workshop model. Replacement filters are between £4 and £5 according to model.

The Microlene is available from **Microclene Filters Ltd**, tel 01705 502999, or numerous suppliers.

Microclene filter with extension tube fitted to provide a more directional airflow

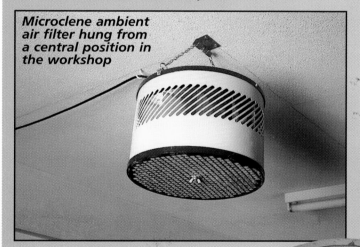

Microclene ambient air filter hung from a central position in the workshop

made from a piece of Perspex and two short lengths of batten. One or two of different height will cater for different depths of cut (*see photo left*).

Ambient air cleaners

While a dust extractor connected to your router will pick up most of the dust, quantities of free dust will be suspended in the workshop atmosphere.

This suspended dust will include the smallest particles – down to one micron or less – which can be the most injurious to health.

I am sufficiently impressed with the Microclene MC1000 ambient air cleaner that I have been testing that I want to buy the review model (*see above*).

Replacement filters for AquaVac extractor and Microclene MC1000 ambient air filter

Safety first

Reducing hazards in the workshop

FOR many readers woodworking is a pleasant and satisfying recreation, but a catalogue of dangers lurk in wait for the unwary which can cast a shadow over their enjoyment.

Safety is a matter of common sense, attention to detail, and concentration. Hazards come in various forms, from unsafe electrical installations to slippery workshop floors, so it pays to know what to look out for and what equipment to get (*see photo 1, below*).

Electrical safety

Many woodworkers use their garage as a workplace, using the 13amp sockets that are usually installed as part of the house wiring.

This is ok, as long as you don't overload the sockets with multi-socket adapters carrying a multitude of plugs.

A multi-way extension lead is a neater way of providing several sockets, and it helps to label each plug to show which one is for which tool.

When you change a router cutter, for example, always unplug the router before handling it. The labelled plugs ensure you unplug the correct tool (*see photo 2*).

If your main power box doesn't have circuit breakers, residual current circuit breakers (RCBs) will protect you against a fault in the wiring.

Check frequently on the state of your plugs and their wiring. Plugs tend to get dropped or dragged over the floor, which can crack them, or pull the wiring out (*see photo 3*).

Solid rubber plugs are better than plastic or ceramic plugs, and fortunately appliances sold for domestic use now have a moulded plug on the end of the cable.

On the subject of plugs, check the fuse is the correct value for the particular tool. Moulded plugs should have the correct fuse, to match the tool, fitted at the factory, but if you buy a standard plug it is likely to come with a 13amp fuse.

Many of your power tools will need only a five or 10amp fuse: anything more doesn't give you the proper level of protection.

▼ *Photo 1 Safety devices are essential when routing; the items shown are a good basic minimum*

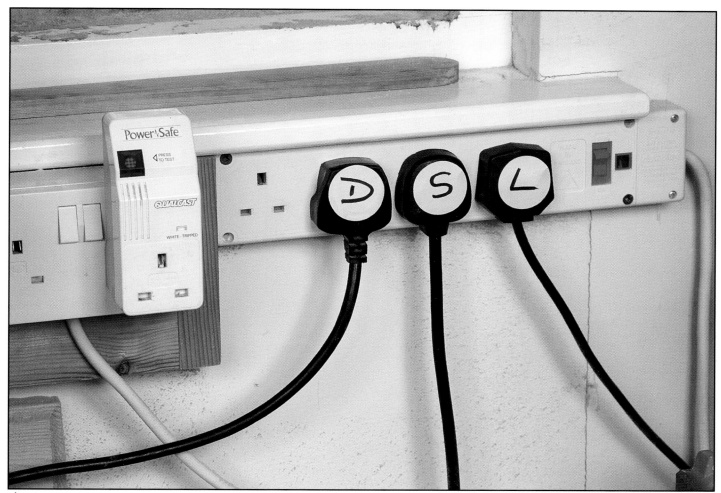

▲ *Photo 2 Plugs labelled to show which plug is for which tool. A contact breaker is in the socket on the left*

If you are building a workshop, or having your shed wired for power-tool work, try to arrange for the power box to be located by the door so you can break the main switch and isolate the whole workshop as you go out (*see photo 4*).

If you are running a power cable down your garden, make sure it's an approved armoured type for outdoor use, and it runs in an approved fashion.

If you're in any doubt get professional advice and installation.

"Make sure there is a clear path to the exit – you might want to leave in a hurry one day"

The workshop

Overcrowded and untidy workshops increase the risk of accidents.

Make sure there is a clear path to the exit – you might want to leave in a hurry one day. Don't let large quantities of shavings and dust accumulate: they are a fire hazard, and things get lost if dropped in them.

If you have a wooden floor, shavings will eventually buff it to a slippery surface. This is exactly what happened in my workshop, in which I used flooring-grade chipboard

Photo 3 This badly wired plug is dangerous and needs the cable to be secured properly

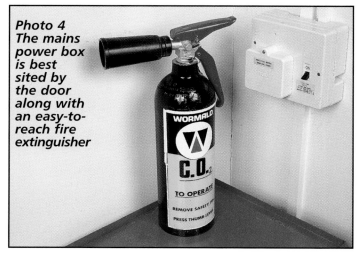

Photo 4 The mains power box is best sited by the door along with an easy-to-reach fire extinguisher

coated with a hard polyurethane varnish. After a few years – even with frequent cleaning – the floor became very slippery. I cured this by coating it with more floor varnish and sprinkling fine sand over the wet varnish with an old flour sifter.

Once dry, I swept up the loose sand and coated the floor with the remainder of the varnish, sealing in the sand. The result is not particularly elegant, but the floor is absolutely non-slip (*see photo 5*).

A fire extinguisher is an essential in the workshop. A type suitable for electrical fires (not water), is required. Learn how to use it and make sure you have it checked at the specified intervals.

Good lighting and a comfortable working temperature help safety. Consider the addition of tungsten lighting, perhaps in the form of spotlights to illuminate the current working position.

Take steps to prevent other people distracting you. Never work with your back to the door, as something as innocent as someone bringing you a cup of tea can take you by surprise, with possibly disastrous effects.

Personal safety gear

Loose clothing can be dangerous, especially the 'warehouse' type coat with patch pockets and wide sleeves, both of which can snag on guards, fences etc.

Woodturning smocks are extremely practical, with zip fastening Velcro cuff straps and pockets at the back. Bulky clothing in cold weather restricts movement and should be avoided.

Protect your feet. Steel-capped shoes beat trainers every time. Tie back long hair, and remove jewellery, rings, medallions on chains and suchlike.

Cover up

Personal protection is mainly a case of looking after the eyes, ears and lungs. Wear safety spectacles or goggles, especially when working with plastic laminates.

Ears are easily protected with ear defenders. These are relatively cheap and very cost-effective, bearing in mind that hearing loss is insidious.

Protect lungs by wearing a facemask and using dust extraction. A moulded facemask which fits round your nose and mouth, and has a breather valve, is among the most practical. They are classified according to the type of dust they protect against.

An effective but more expensive way of protecting eyes and lungs simultaneously is with a full-face, battery-powered respirator such as the Racal Airlite (*see photo 6*).

▶ *Photo 6 Me adopting a comfortable position for routing, wearing ear defenders and 'Airlite' helmet; edge moulding with dust extraction fixed to router*

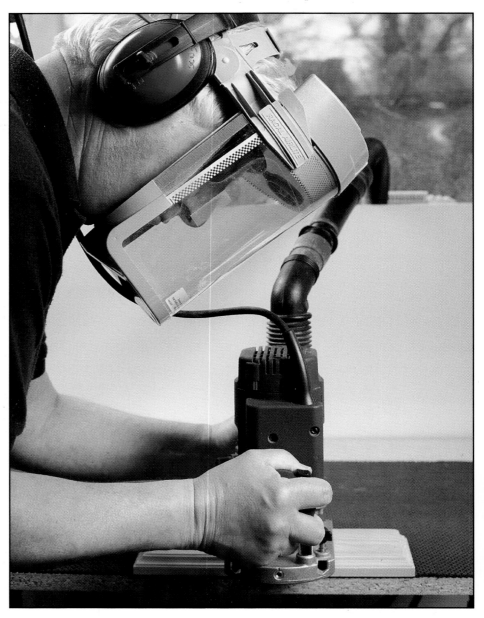

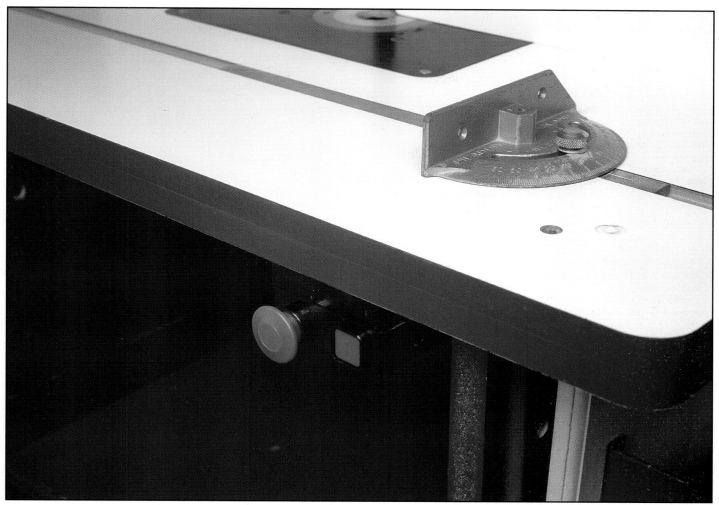

▲ *Photo 7 NVR switch on table, positioned so that it can be easily switched off with a thigh*

In these, a stream of filtered air is blown down over the face and out at the bottom of the mask. They are excellent for spectacle wearers because they keep your lenses clear, unlike some of the other types of goggles.

Dust extraction

Use dust extraction wherever possible. Many current routers have dust extraction spouts added as an afterthought. These are far from perfect, but still worth using.

The two best routers for dust extraction are the Festo 1000EB and the Elu97/DeWalt DW621, which have built-in dust extraction, making them easier to use as well as more effective.

"Try to work in a good light, and never when you are tired or ill"

Using the router

Try to work in a good light, and never when you are tired or ill.

Create a working routine – router unplugged; cutter inserted in collet; check the collet nut has been tightened; all fastenings on router are properly tightened; all guards fitted and secured.

If necessary make a checklist. If you always go through the same check procedures, they will become ingrained into your working practices.

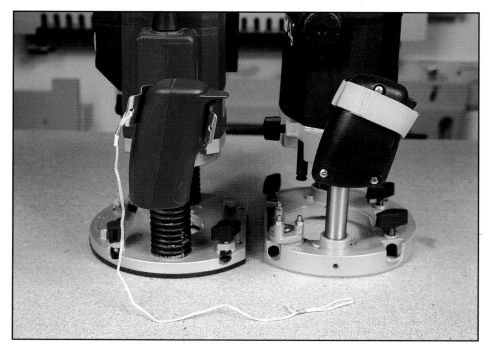

◄ *Photo 8 Switch clip on Bosch GOF1300 router, Velcro strap on Trend T9*

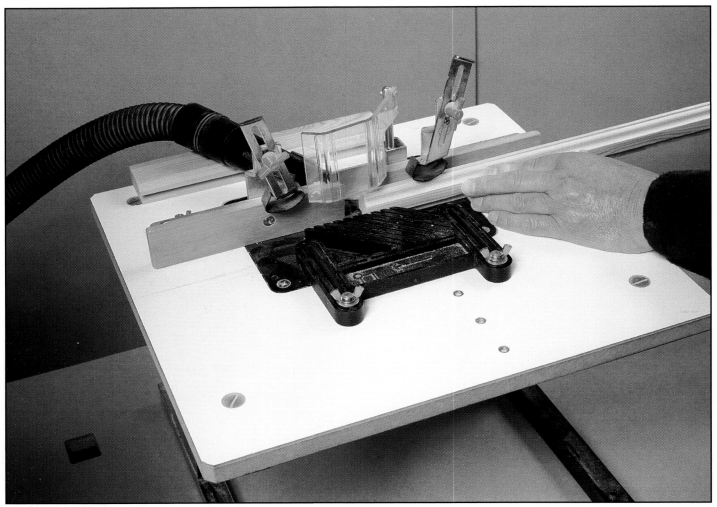

▲ *Photo 9 Guards in use for safe table routing*

Cutters

Cutters can be dangerous long before they are put in the router. Some makes are shipped tightly-held in containers, making it difficult to extract them. Use an old gardening glove or similar to protect your hands.

The glove also comes in handy the first time you remove the tight factory-fitted Allen screw that holds the bearing on a bearing-guided cutter.

Follow your router instructions on inserting cutters – at least three-quarters of shank length inside the collet – and keep them sharp. A chattering cutter is a sign of wear or dirt.

Make sure your cutter is clear of the workpiece before you switch the router on. A large cutter in contact with the wood could knock the router out of your hand.

At the end of the cut keep concentrating. The relief at having completed the cut can cause you to relax and knock the corner of your workpiece, or worse.

"A chattering cutter is a sign of wear or dirt"

Make sure the cutter has stopped revolving before attempting to remove it.

Keep your collet clean and keep an eye on it for wear (*see page 12*).

▼ *Photo 10 Combined guard/dust extractor for table when fence is not in use*

"The price of safety is eternal vigilance"

Adopt a proper stance when working. Don't stand too far back, feet wide apart, knees locked, arms straight, fists clenched, jaws clenched, eyes narrowed.

The correct stance is the simple 'sports stance'. One foot a little in front of the other, body leaning forward slightly, elbows slightly bent. This gives balance and enables you to move your body behind the cut, extending the arms as you go.

Router table use

Using the router inverted in a table can be a safer process than hand-held routing, but a number of extra precautions have to be taken.

Wherever possible operate your router via a No Volt Release (NVR) switch mounted on the table. If you haven't got one, use the router switch rather than the mains socket.

An increasing number of routers are now fitted with 'safety' switches which cannot be locked on. These should be clipped or strapped 'on' for table use.

Don't use elastic bands, bits of old inner tube or plastic garden ties. These are unsafe and, in commercial workshops, illegal. The switch restraint should be capable of being freed quickly in an emergency.

A router cutter rotates in an anti-clockwise direction as you look at it in a table. Always feed the workpiece from right to left, and never try a 'reverse cut' such as you might occasionally use in hand-held routing.

Always use guards and pressure pads when table routing (*see photo 9*) and always use a push-stick for narrow work.

With most router tables, both commercial and home-made, the guards, holddowns and dust extraction point are part of the fence.

If you remove the fence, such as for pattern moulding with a bearing-guided cutter, you also remove the guards and dust extraction. An exception is the Veritas table, where the table top is steel and the dust spout is held with magnets, independently of the fence.

A combined guard/dust extractor can be very easily made from Perspex and batten (*see photo 10*). A lead-in pin overcomes the need to push the workpiece straight on to the cutter. In the absence of a pin a piece of batten with the end rounded can be clamped to the table top.

Box-maker's jig

Very small components are inherently easier to rout on a table, but your fingers are close to the cutter. Many small components can be machined using a combined guard/guide, often referred to as a 'box-maker's jig' (*see photo 11*).

This is a simple right-angle fixture that steers the workpiece and keeps the fingers away from the cutter. It also does away with the need for a mitre fence, and so the need to align the router fence parallel with the mitre fence slot when using the mitre fence.

The final word

This chapter has highlighted some of the major aspects of health and safety when using your router. I haven't told you anything you didn't already know, but you must apply it. To misquote a well-known saying "the price of safety is eternal vigilance".

Photo 11 Small box-ends being routed with box-maker's jig, keeps the fingers safe

Kitting up for under £200

Setting up a beginner routing system with room for expansion

THE recreational woodworker has always been rather put off routing by the initial cost of setting up, but in the last year or two the situation has been transformed.

Three factors have brought down the cost of setting up a routing system: the availability of several inexpensive, well-

made medium-duty routers; the proliferation of extraordinarily cheap boxed sets of cutters; and the development of a number of small, relatively inexpensive, router tables.

This article presents my choice of a system within a total budget of £200. It is not the cheapest available, but I

believe it represents the best value for money, taking into account its immediate capabilities and its scope for future expansion.

Above all, it is not just another 'ideal for beginners' kit, to be scrapped when said beginners can afford something better.

▼ *The components of the system – table, router, cutters, hone*

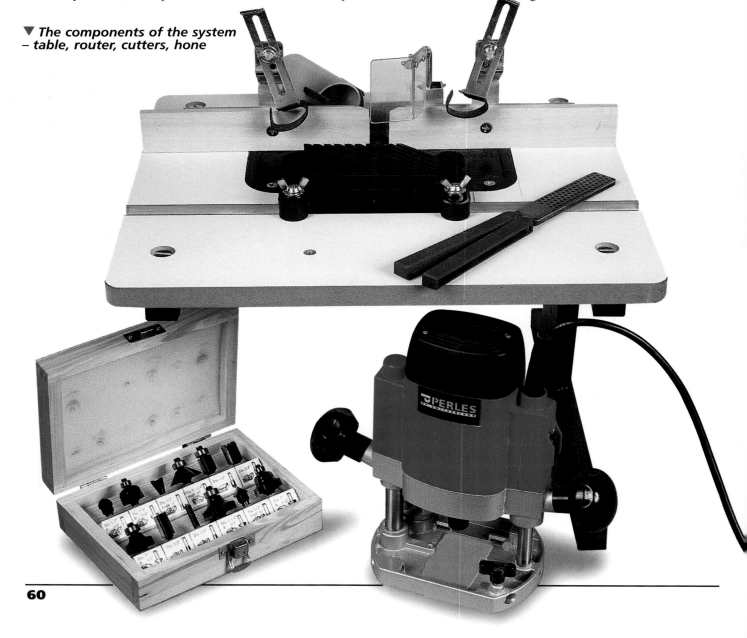

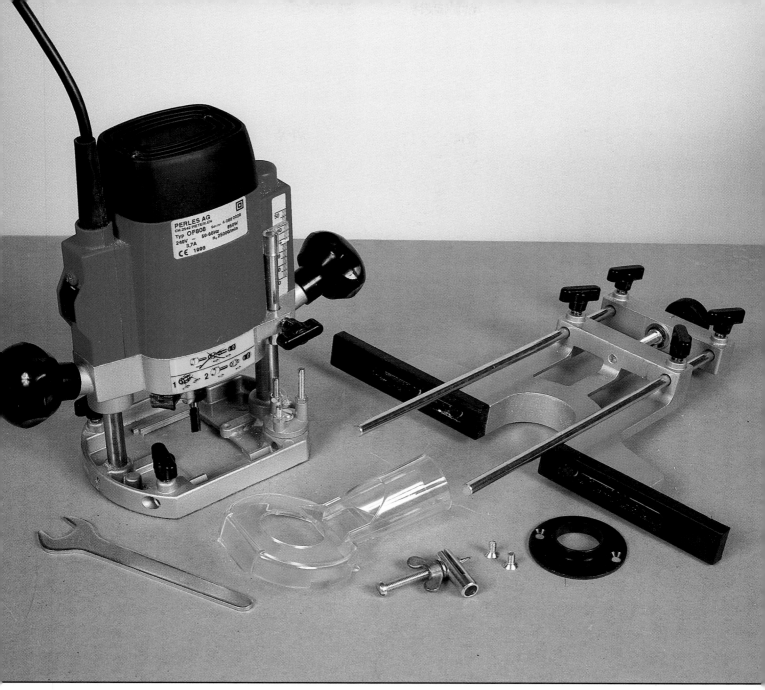

Router

I have chosen the Perles OF 808 single-speed model, which comes with side fence, 30mm guide bush, beam-trammel attachment for curved and circular work, and transparent plastic dust-extractor spout.

The side fence is fitted with a micro adjuster and sliding plastic cheeks. A ¼in multi-slit collet is supplied as standard and an 8mm collet is available as an optional extra.

The OF 808 is currently available at a discounted price of around £100 from The Woodcut Trading Company among other companies (*trade magazines usually list contacts*).

▲ *The Perles router with standard accessories*

"It is not just another 'ideal for beginners' kit, to be scrapped when said beginners can afford something better"

This router is compatible with many of the accessories and attachments made for the late lamented Elu 96, so giving tremendous scope for expansion. Its 850W

motor is capable of driving quite big cutters without the need for variable speed.

The base plate has two tapped 6mm holes in exactly the same position as on the old Elu, making it very easy to attach the router to the insert plate of a router table, and also allowing the use of other attachments.

The simple slider switch presents no problem when using the router inverted in a table.

"This router is compatible with many of the accessories and attachments made for the late lamented Elu 96"

"While not of industrial quality, these Chinese-made cutters are capable of a lot of work at the 'domestic' level provided they are kept clean, and sharpened with a diamond hone"

Cutters

I have selected the WTC-1412 12-piece boxed set from The Woodcut Trading Company. These ¼in shank TCT cutters

▼ *Table with router mounted and dust extractor connected*

Costs breakdown

The best prices I found at the time of writing are given below, but the market is extremely volatile at the moment and better – or worse – bargains might be on offer when you are seeking to buy.

Item	Price
Router	£ 79.95
Cutters	£ 18.95
Table	£ 76.00
Hone	£ 16.00
Total	£190.90

This keeps us inside our budget but excludes dust extraction; see below, an NVR switch, and a mitre fence.
Note: You might find a package deal on the router plus box of cutters at a within-budget price.

Dust extraction
The budget of £200 does not allow for the purchase of a dust extractor, but if you already have a suitable vacuum cleaner, the router and the table both provide for dust extraction.
With this system I use the AquaVac Synchro 30A. Cheaper vacuum cleaners can be bought from about £50 but are not as efficient.
You will also need an adapter to couple the vacuum hose to the router and table spouts. Mine is from Draper and costs about £4.
Adding dust extraction from scratch will put at least £50 on your costs, but it will also cater for any other power tool fitted with an extractor spout.

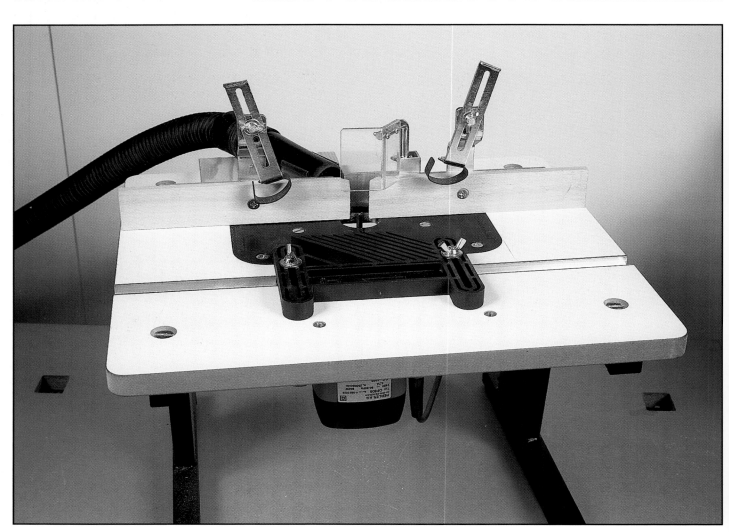

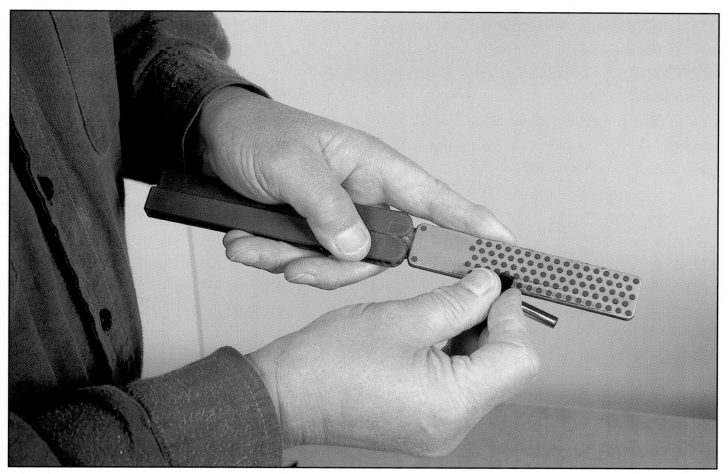

▲ *Honing a bearing-guided cutter (bearing removed)* ▼ *Cutting an arc using the trammel point*

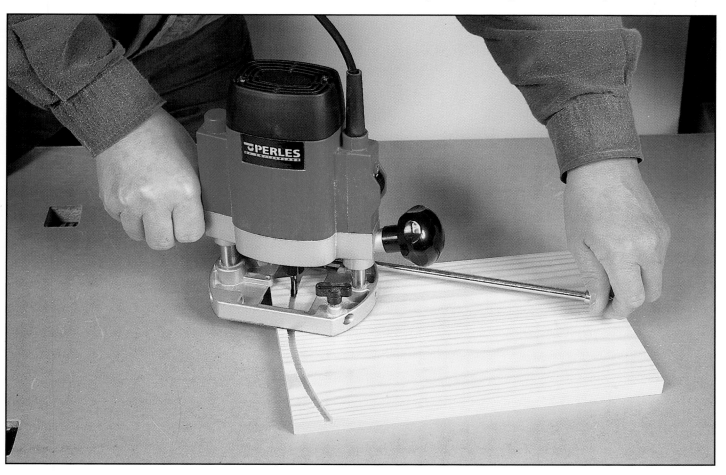

▲ *Examples of items made with the system and just using cutters from the budget box – key cupboard, kitchen list, circles*

"My system will expand with your needs without having to buy a new router or table"

cost a remarkable £18.95 including VAT and delivery.

While not of industrial quality, these Chinese-made cutters are capable of a lot of work at the 'domestic' level provided

Bending the budget

You could save around £30 on the router by buying the Power Devil PDW 5027 for a rock-bottom budget kit.

You could also save around £20 by buying the new Charnwood W001 table; the top fits over the pegs in a Workmate, but is nowhere near as convenient as the freestanding model.

If you want a more upmarket set of cutters, consider spending another £70 on Wealden's boxed set of carefully chosen shapes and sizes.

Finally, if you were looking ahead to such delights as panelled-door making you could consider spending another £30 to buy the Perles variable-speed 'soft start' OF 808E router.

This would enable you to reduce motor speed for larger diameter cutters and also to cut plastics and alloys at the correct speeds for these materials.

they are kept clean, and sharpened with a diamond hone. The Woodcut Trading Company has a suitable folding-handle style of this essential item for £18.95 – their super-fine grade hone (colour coded green), model number MM-D1SF.

As with most boxed sets, in practice you get more than 12 different cutters. Two of the five bearings in the set are ¼in outside diameter and three are ½in.

By switching bearings you can change the effect of the cut, rounding-over cutters, for example, becoming ovolos with the smaller bearing, and the profiles of the Roman ogee and cove cutters altering when the larger bearing is fitted.

In addition, different effects can be produced by varying the depth of cut of cutters such as the Roman ogee.

The bearings can be removed with a 1.5mm Allen key.

Table

The little Charnwood W002/Woodcut Trading Company 999-200 table – which I have been using for the past five years – retails at around £76 and is available from the Woodcut Trading Company or any Charnwood stockist.

The table is bench-standing, with rubber feet which enable it to be placed on a level surface of suitable height without clamping.

A basic, but adequate, fence is provided, along with a clear plastic shield, simple hold-downs, and plastic feather board for guarding the fingers and guiding the work.

An alloy mitre fence slot is built in, but the mitre fence itself is an optional accessory. A dust extractor spout of 50mm (2in) plastic is attached behind the fence with a spring clip.

The router insert plate is made of 8mm (⅝₆in) high-density plastic with a cutter aperture of 35mm (1⅜in). The router attachment holes are sufficiently wide apart to make it possible to enlarge this aperture if required.

Fixing holes for the router have to be drilled by the user; the Perles OF 808 requires two countersunk holes to take 6mm machine screws. The extra gained by drilling ¼in holes provides comfortable clearance for 6mm screws.

An NVR switch would add about £35 to the cost, but could be left for future expansion.

Expansion

My budget system should enable you to do most of the routing you are ever likely to require, unless you progress to heavy-duty work demanding high-power ½in variable-speed routers with cutters and table to match.

At some stage, however, you are bound to want to tackle dovetailing, biscuit jointing, ellipse cutting, and possibly even lathe work with a device such as the Trend Routerlathe. My system will expand with your needs without having to buy a new router or table.

The most obvious starting place for expansion is the purchase of additional cutters for specific tasks. No matter what boxed set you start with, sooner or later you will need to buy particular cutters for particular jobs.

For an essential, but rarely repeated job a medium-priced cutter, from say the Titan or Wealden range, will be more than adequate, whereas for constant use – principally with straights – you might well decide to buy a premium-quality cutter such as CMT or Titman.

You could take advantage of the increasing range of 8mm shank cutters by buying the optional 8mm collet for your router. If so, do invest in an extra collet nut so that each collet can live in its own nut.

As soon as you start table work you will appreciate the value of a fine-height adjuster to set the depth of cut.

Better still would be the WoodRat PlungeBar. This will completely transform your table routing by enabling you to plunge and lock your router at the required depth of cut almost as easily as you can do it by hand. For the Perles OF 808 models the Universal B model is the one, price £24.95.

Beyond this, a vast range of accessories is available to fit the OF 808. These include additional guidebushes, dovetail jigs, circle and ellipse jigs.

By choosing your initial set-up wisely, you can expand without any of your original components having to be replaced.

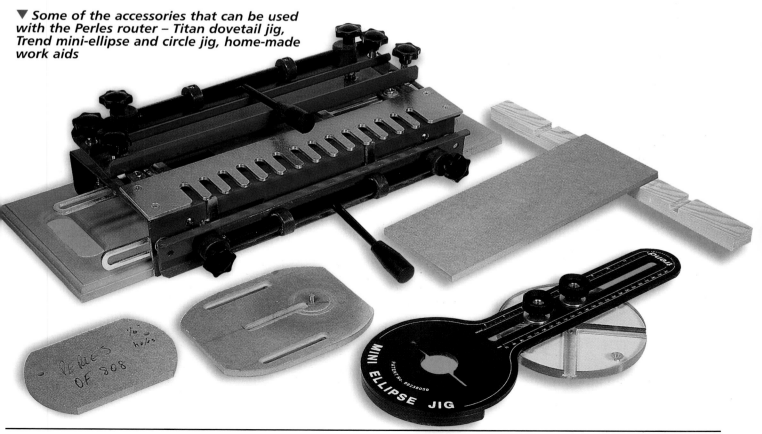

▼ *Some of the accessories that can be used with the Perles router – Titan dovetail jig, Trend mini-ellipse and circle jig, home-made work aids*

Checking the tightness of the bearing on a bearing-guided cutter

A guiding hand

Making friends with your guidebushes

A GUIDEBUSH is one of the standard accessories supplied with virtually all routers, but reaction from my course students suggests that in many cases it remains undiscovered and unused. This is a great pity because guidebushes, used with templates, open up a whole area of creative routing (*see photo 1*).

The guidebush is essentially a circular flange, usually between l0mm and 40mm, projecting from the router base. The cutter plunges through the middle of the bush, and the edge of the flange runs against the edge of a template to reproduce the shape of the template.

Because the cutter is smaller in diameter than the bush, the cut in the workpiece is offset some distance from the edge of the template. This offset has to be allowed for when making the template and is calculated as: $\frac{1}{2} \times$ (outside diameter of guidebush minus the diameter of cutter). Thus, with a guidebush of 24mm diameter and a cutter of 8mm, the offset will be $\frac{1}{2} \times (24 - 8) = 8$mm. The *Trend Routing Catalogue* contains, on page 127, a ready-reckoner table showing the offsets for various combinations of guidebush and cutter (*and see fig 1 for the essentials of guidebush theory*).

Example

As an example of guidebush work we shall rout a hand-hold in a piece of MDF. The template is made of 9mm MDF which is comfortably deeper than the 96E guidebush flange.

▲ *Photo 1 Array of routers and guidebushes*

A 24mm guidebush is used with a ¼in straight cutter, giving an offset of 8.8mm. The template should therefore be 8.8mm bigger all round than the required hole.

The workpiece is taped to the cutting table with heavy-duty double-sided carpet tape and the template taped to the workpiece. A piece of tape under the centre of the workpiece helps prevent the waste jumping around as the final cut is made (*see photo 2*).

After cutting the hole, its top edge is decorated, a small bearing-guided ovolo giving a finished look.

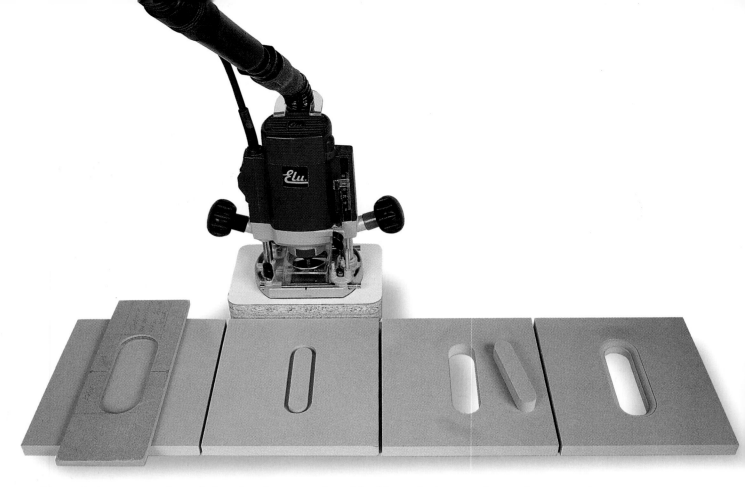

▲ *Photo 2 Sequence, from left – Ready to cut hand-hold workpiece and template taped to cutting table, 96E with guidebush and cutter in, dust extraction fitted; making the cut, half-way through; the finished cut, scrap lifted out and placed on top of workpiece; the final hand-hold decorated with a small ovolo cutter*

Templates

Making templates need not be difficult. For the simple template described above, I just laid my hand on the MDF to judge how big the hole should be, then cut two circles with the appropriate size of hole saw.

I then joined the circles with two straight cuts with the router and straight edge.

"To reduce the size of the hole, just increase the diameter of the guidebush, so that the offset becomes larger and the hole smaller"

Hand-hold sizes

By way of a simple introduction to the creative use of guidebushes, note that one of my mounting boards is so narrow that the combination of guidebush and cutter used above would have produced a hole longer than the width of the board.

To reduce the size of the hole, just increase the diameter of the guidebush, so that the offset becomes larger and the hole smaller.

I cut two hand-holds in a board with two different guidebushes, the same template and ¼in cutter – demonstrating the value of having a range of guidebush sizes (*see photo 5*).

Availability

The biggest choice of guidebushes is found in the Trend T9 and T5, Elu 96 and 97 and Hitachi ranges. The Elu 97 and the Bosch 900 and 1300 have state-of-the-art bushes.

◀ *Photo 3 Trend sub-base kit for adapting routers to use the Trend Elu 96 range of guidebushes*

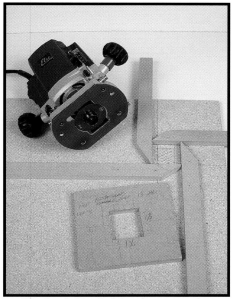

▲ Photo 4 Straight edges used as a template to cut holes in cutting table. The template, made with these straight edges, is also shown

▶Photo 5 Two different size hand-holds cut with the same template and cutter but using different guidebushes

"If your router manufacturer does not offer a comprehensive set of guidebushes, a sub-base can be bought or made"

Elu 97 bushes are made in skeleton form to maintain the high standard of dust extraction that comes with this model. Bosch 900 and 1300 bushes have a quick-release bayonet fitting, but the range is not as wide as that of Elu and Hitachi models.

False router base

If your router manufacturer does not offer a comprehensive set of guidebushes, a sub-base can be bought or made to take, say, the Elu 96 range of bushes.

A commercial sub-base available from Trend comes ready-drilled to fit the Elu 177 routers, which also cover the Bosch l600 and 1700 models. (*See also page 81.*)

For those with other routers, specify the model when ordering and Trend will drill the appropriate holes and supply the fixings.

The sub-base takes Elu 96 guidebushes. These are available in 12 different sizes, from 12mm outside diameter to 40mm. A thirteenth, of 10mm OD, is supplied as part of a cutter centring kit.

The sub-base takes another 8mm of your depth of cut away, but is useful if you need a range of guidebushes not supplied by your router manufacturer.

The Trend sub-base (*see photo 3*) is drilled for the Elu 177E and the Bosch 900 ACE, together with the centring kit.

Long cutters

The thickness of the template and the use of a sub-base reduce depth of cut. This can be a serious problem with some routers, but fortunately much template work involves cutting with straight cutters; Titman and Trend supply special long-shank cutters for the purpose, Titman calling them 'long reach cutters' and Trend naming theirs 'pocket cutters'.

Alternatively, buy the straight cutters made for the Leigh Dovetail Jig. Their extra-long shanks cater for the thickness of the Leigh dovetail comb, and can be obtained from most cutter suppliers.

"Any straight-sided figure, internal or external, can be cut by using a number of straight edges"

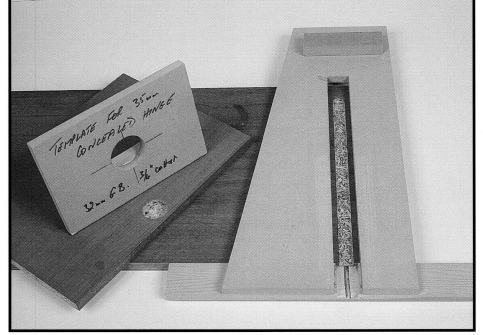

◀ Photo 6 Stopped housing being cut with a simple jig using a guide-bush, plus hinge-sinking jig with example of hole

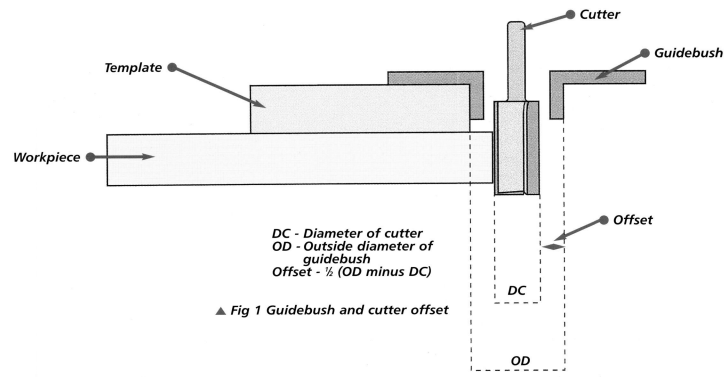

Template ●

Cutter ●

Guidebush ●

Workpiece ●

Offset ●

DC - Diameter of cutter
OD - Outside diameter of
 guidebush
Offset - ½ (OD minus DC)

DC

OD

▲ *Fig 1 Guidebush and cutter offset*

More on templates

Many guidebush applications do not require a specific template. Any straight-sided figure, internal or external, can be cut by using a number of straight edges, one for each side of the figure.

A set of four MDF straight edges are shown used as a template for the fixing holes in my sacrificial cutting table (*see photo 4*). The rectangle for each hole is marked on the table and a second rectangle drawn around the first with the particular offset required by the bush/cutter combination.

The straight edges are tacked or taped along the perimeter of this outer rectangle and the cut made with several passes. The chisel-shaped ends of the straight edges allow a wide swing of angle (*see photo 4*).

After you have cut one or two figures with the above set-up it will dawn on you that the straight edges can equally be used to make a template.

My sacrificial tables are actually cut with the template shown (*see photo 4*). To make it, take a piece of 9mm or 12mm MDF and mark on it the two rectangles (*see Fig 1*).

Now draw a third rectangle outside the second, offset by the same distance as the second from the first. Tape your straight edges to this outer rectangle, make your cut and the result is a template to provide the desired size of hole.

There is no need to square the rounded inside corners. Use of a ¼in cutter will ensure that their radius will be smaller than that of the smallest guidebush (*see Fig 2*).

Similar tricks can be used to carefully make more elaborate templates – but remember to write on each template its purpose and what guidebushes and cutters it is used with.

▼ *Fig 2 Using straight edges to make a template*

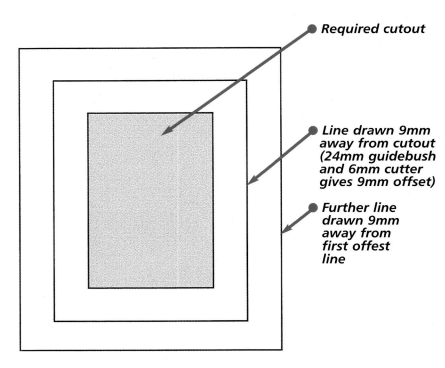

Required cutout ●

Line drawn 9mm away from cutout (24mm guidebush and 6mm cutter gives 9mm offset) ●

Further line drawn 9mm away from first offest line ●

Other uses

Guidebushes also have an important role in cutting housings. A simple housing jig, in which the router is guided by a guidebush running in a groove, not only enables the cut to be positioned accurately but also prevents the router deviating from the cut.

A further simple application is sinking concealed hinges in cabinet doors. A jig consisting of an accurately cut circle is used with a guidebush and straight cutter. The diameter of the circle is dependent on the guidebush and cutter to be used. A batten fixes the distance of the hole from the edge of the door (*see photo 6*).

A simple housing jig with a stop taped to it will satisfactorily cut a stopped housing, but for a more sophisticated version, refer to Roy Sutton's book, *Jig Making for the Router*.

Table chop

Creating a cutting table

THE newcomer to routing soon discovers that often the hardest part of a job is holding the work-piece. There are two aspects to this problem:

What to hold it with

What to hold it on

The second aspect is less obvious than the first. More than one enthusiast has cut into an expensive workbench before realising the need for a sacrificial cutting table.

What's needed is a simple double-sided table that sits on top of a Workmate or similar portable bench, and supports the workpiece.

If a job needs a cut right through the workpiece, the cut can be made into the sacrificial cutting table without damaging a valuable bench top, and without having to improvise a false top.

The cutting table (*see photo 1*) is by far the most heavily used work aid in my workshop. Its construction needs only a light-duty router and one straight TCT cutter, plus a simple template and guide-bush.

> "The cutting table is by far the most heavily used work aid in my workshop"

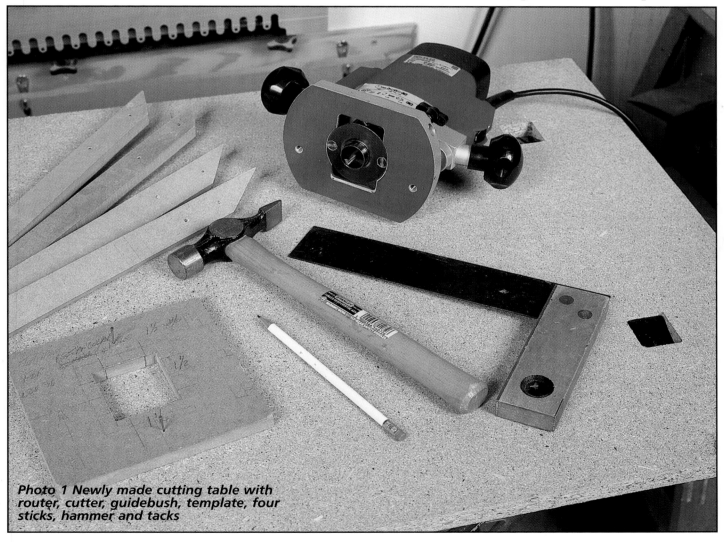

Photo 1 Newly made cutting table with router, cutter, guidebush, template, four sticks, hammer and tacks

Photo 2 New board
marked for the position
of clamp holes

Materials

The table is made from a piece of chipboard about 19mm (¾in) thick. The dimensions are not critical, except that the board should be thick enough to clear the top of the Workmate clamping pegs that will hold it.

Some portable bench vices, for example the Richmond and later model Workmates, have thicker pegs than the older Workmates, so tables to fit these will have to be correspondingly thicker.

You could use a piece of kitchen worktop for this, or glue two pieces of chipboard together.

Photo 3 Tacking the template to the piece of chipboard for the cutting table

When making my original table I covered one side with 4mm (³⁄₁₆in) hardboard. This provides a smoother surface for use with double-sided adhesive tape, and gives a more sympathetic surface for cutting into.

These days I don't bother with the hardboard, which saves both time and money, but it could bring the chipboard up to thickness if you have a bench with thicker pegs.

Construction

Start by preparing a rectangle of chipboard. It needs to be comfortably larger than the Workmate top with the jaws fully extended. This enables clamps to be used all round the edge. I bought the piece for my table as a ready-cut panel, 915 by 610mm (36 by 24in).

Make sure the edges are clean and square, and the corners right-angled, as you will use them occasionally to guide your router fence when using the table. If the panel is not a perfect rectangle, use your router with a straight edge to square it off.

Place the pegs in the four corner positions of your Workmate. Open the jaws to their full extent, then close them by about 10mm (⅜in) to give yourself the necessary range of movement when fitting the finished table.

Mark the positions of the four rectangular holes by placing the board against the pegs, first to set the end (short side) positions, then the front and back (long side) positions.

Draw pencil lines to form a grid and mark the holes at the intersections of the grid (*see photo 2*). The size of the holes is not critical as long as they are big enough to accommodate the plastic peg tops.

Err towards making them too big, as this will make fitting the table to the Workmate easier.

"As it's a knock-about table don't worry about putting pinholes in its surface"

Template

Cut the clamp holes with whatever you have at your disposal, a jigsaw, padsaw, drill and rasp etc. As this is a routing table I thought it fitting to use the router with a ¼in straight cutter.

This involves using simple guidebush techniques, which calls for a template. For my first table I made a simple template from 12mm MDF.

Select the guidebush and cutter. I used a ¼in straight TCT cutter with a 24mm guidebush. This combination gives an offset of 9mm.

Photo 4 Routing a clamp hole using the template

Since the size of the clamp holes need not be precise as long as they are big enough, we can round up the 9mm to 10mm to give ourselves some leeway.

Make the template by drawing the size of the hole needed on a piece of 12mm MDF. Draw a second rectangle around the first, set 10mm outside the original rectangle, then

cut the larger hole with a fretsaw or jigsaw.

Clamp the chipboard to the Workmate, with the position of the clamp hole to be cut over the gap between the jaws. Fasten the template over this hole with double-sided tape, hot-melt glue or pins (*see photo 3*). As it's a knockabout table don't worry about putting pinholes in its surface.

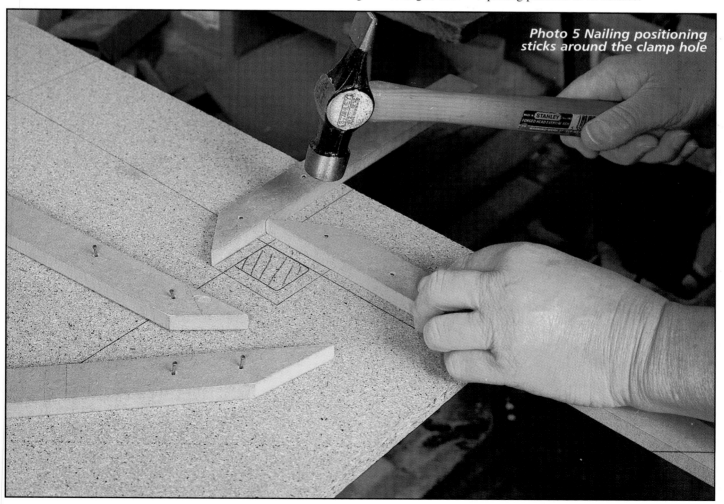

Photo 5 Nailing positioning sticks around the clamp hole

Cut the hole in a series of light cuts (*see photo 4*) no more than about 4mm at a time, particularly if using a light-duty router. Move clockwise around the inside of the template to keep the right cutting direction.

Keep going until the chipboard is cut right through. Carefully lever the template off the workpiece with a chisel, taking care not to damage either of the two surfaces, and proceed in the same manner for the other three holes.

Sticks

An alternative to making a template is to

"On a variable speed router, lower the speed to about 18,000rpm to reduce chipboard burning"

use four straight sticks of 9 or 12mm MDF. These will form our 'template'.

Make the sticks about 50mm (2in) wide and about 300mm (12in) long, again, exact size is not important.

Cut the ends of the sticks in a chisel shape to make it easier to fit them to various angled shapes. Keep them for future

use – you will find them useful for routing any straight-sided figure.

To use the sticks, draw the outlines of the four clamping holes (actual size) on the workpiece. Draw a larger box around each one, set away from the edges of the first by the exact amount of the guide-bush/cutter offset.

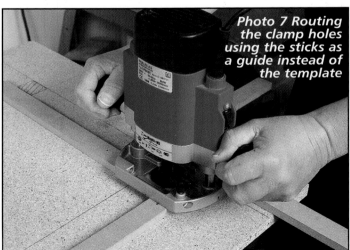

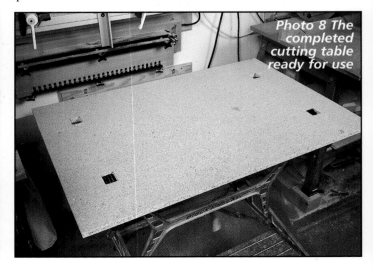

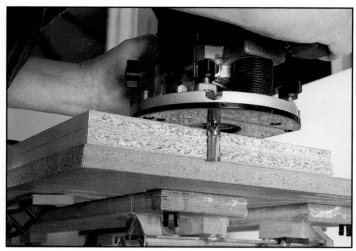

▲ Photo 9 Workpieces being cut while clamped to cutting table to preserve the bench's surface

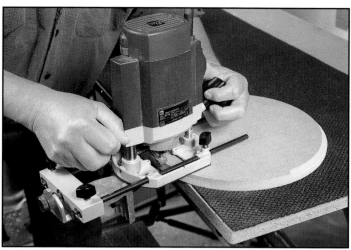

▲ Photo 10 An arc being cut in panel while the workpiece is held to cutting table with double-sided tape

Position the sticks around the larger box and pin to the workpiece (*see photos 5 and 6*) routing as with the template (*see photo 7*).

Whichever method you use, try to move the router steadily without hesitating at the corners. With chipboard, too slow a cut results in burnt edges and a poor finish.

If you have a variable-speed router, lower the speed to about 18,000rpm. This is a useful trick with chipboard to reduce burning.

"Try to move the router steadily without hesitating at the corners"

The hole is smaller than the outline of the template because of the offset, and the sharpness of the corners depends solely on the diameter of the cutter; it has nothing to do with the diameter of the guidebush. This often comes as a surprise to the beginner.

Straight edge template

After you have made one or two cutting tables it will probably dawn on you that you can use the sticks to make the template, which will speed up the making of subsequent tables. To do so, take a piece

Photo 11 The large flat surface of the cutting table makes an ideal platform for router mats

of 9 or 12 mm MDF and draw three rectangles on it.

Rectangle 1 is the actual cut-out you are making, in this case 32 × 38mm (1¼ × 1½in).

Rectangle 2 is drawn the distance of your guidebush/cutter offset around the first rectangle, in our case 9mm, or 10mm for luck.

Rectangle 3 is drawn a further 10mm from the second rectangle to allow for the guidebush/cutter offset on the template (*see fig 1*).

Tack or tape the four sticks around the outside rectangle, make your cut and you will have cut a hole, which in turn will give you the required hole for the Workmate pegs.

Your first thought might be to square the rounded corners of your new template, but this isn't necessary if you use a narrow cutter.

With a ¼in cutter, the radius of each corner will be smaller than the radius of the smallest guidebush you are likely to use, so the bush will cut across the corner of the template.

The trick of using straight edges to make a template has numerous applications. It is particularly useful for inside cuts, such as in the template for the cutting table. Outside cuts are equally easy, but you can usually make them with simpler methods if necessary.

Using the cutting table

To use the table, place the pegs in the corners of the Workmate, open the jaws, drop the finished table (*see photo 8*) over the pegs and tighten the jaws.

You will find yourself using the table all the time, for all sorts of work (*see photos 9, 10 and 11*) and will find many new uses.

Eventually both sides will become heavily cut and scarred with use. That is why you made it in the first place. As it approaches this stage, make another one ready for when your current one has to be scrapped (*see photo 12*).

▲ **Photo 12 A well-used cutting table. When both sides look like this it is time to make a new one**

"The trick of using straight edges to make a template has numerous applications"

For my latest tables I bought a 4 × 3ft panel of chipboard for £4.70. I cut it in two to make two 3 × 2ft cutting tables. Each took no more than half an hour to make at a cost of £2.35 each. Not bad for the most useful of all the work aids you will ever make.

▼ *Fig 1 Using straight edges to make a template*

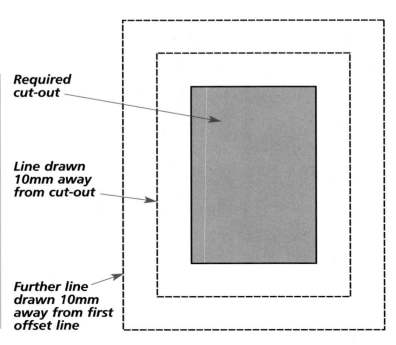

Required cut-out

Line drawn 10mm away from cut-out

Further line drawn 10mm away from first offset line

Cutter/guidebush offsets

To remind you of the calculation, the offset i.e. the distance that the cut takes place from the edge of the template, is given by:

(Outside diameter of guidebush – diameter of cutter) ÷ 2.

If we think of our ¼in as 6mm to make the arithmetic easier, this gives us:

(24mm - 6mm) ÷ 2 = 18 ÷ 2 = 9mm.

Guidebush buster

▲ *Routers, a selection of guidebushes, some long-reach cutters, and a home-made router stand*

Getting to grips with guidebushes so you can tell the good from the great

AMONG the many accessories available for the router, guidebushes are one of the most useful. In this chapter I'll explore the range available, and show how guidebushes can be interchanged between models or home-made for particular routers.

Guidebushes

Most router manufacturers include a guidebush as part of the standard kit, but not all provide an additional range as accessories. A wide range is provided by DeWalt for the DW621 series and these are specific to the routers, being made in skeleton form, apart from the two largest because of their narrower flanges, to retain the excellent dust extraction of the DW621.

Hitachi also offer a wide range, and Hitachi guidebushes fit any one of the Hitachi models, the ZK 2008, M8V and M12V.

Trend, however, provide the largest range of all, with thirteen different diameters which fit both the T5 and the T9, and a further three large-diameter bushes – 50mm, 60mm and 70mm – for the T9 only. A very useful feature is that the size is clearly marked on each bush. On top of this there are bushes for specific accessories such as dovetail or letter-box jigs.

A number of other medium-power routers accept the Trend T5 range of guidebushes. These include the DeWalt 613, Perles OF 808/E, HolzHer 2356, Atlas Copco OFSE 1000, Einhell EOF 850, and Power Devil PDW 850. This is extremely useful when you want to extend your range of bushes, since the Trend T5 bushes are the most widely available.

With some of the Trend-compatible routers, the Trend guidebushes, or their screw-heads, stand proud of the router base, because some bases have too shallow a recess. This presents no problem; all that

is necessary is to make a false base plate of Formica or similar material and fasten it to the router base with double-sided tape. This deepens the recess by raising the base by a small amount.

The photo on page 79 shows some of the other routers which will take the Trend standard bushes.

"Most router manufacturers include a guidebush as part of the standard kit"

Trend, Elu and Hitachi

The Trend, Elu and Hitachi guidebushes happen to be exactly the same diameter,

▲ The DeWalt DW621
router with its complete
set of guidebushes

but their modes of fitting are slightly different so they are not directly interchangeable. However, they can easily be made so; by drilling two holes in the

Hitachi or filing two notches in the Trend.

The benefit of this is that one set of bushes can cover a Hitachi plus any one of the Trend-compatible routers.

Trend to Hitachi

Place the Trend bush in the Hitachi router with the Trend fixing holes at 90° to the Hitachi fixing points. Scratch the positions

▼ The Trend T5 and T9 routers with Trend guidebushes, including the three large bushes for the T9, with inner plate and centring pin

▼ *Routers which take the Trend bushes, the home-made Formica sub-base gives the guidebush screws clearance*

of the required notches on the Trend bush by reference to the screw holes in the base of the Hitachi router.

If you already have one of each – you should have if you have got a Hitachi router – tape them together and scratch round the Hitachi fixing points to mark the positions on the Trend bush. Cut, grind or file the notches and clean off any burr.

The filed notches do not have to be absolutely precise because the bush is positioned by the recess machined in the router base rather than by the fixing points.

▼ *A selection of modified Trend and Hitachi bushes*

"Cut, grind or file the notches and clean off any burr"

Hitachi to Trend

Mark the position of the two required holes either from the Trend router base or by taping one of each type of bush together. Drill and countersink two 6mm holes. As before, the bush is located in the recess in

the router base, so slightly over will not affect the accuracy of the fit.

Bush benefits

Apart from the obvious benefits of one set of bushes fitting more than one router, and the fact that the Trend range is the most widely available, there is the major benefit to owners of Hitachi, HolzHer and other models, of being able to buy accessories such as the DeWalt, Titan and Trend dovetail jigs, and use the bush that comes with them, or quickly adapt it.

With the much more sophisticated Leigh dovetail jig, adaptor plates to take the standard Leigh bushes are available for virtually every make and model of router.

One further point. With routers such as the Trend T5, Perles 808, and HolzHer 2356, the collet can be plunged through the base plate. The best models for this are the HolzHer 2356 and Atlas Copco OF 1000.

This feature is extremely useful when using the router with a guidebush for template work because it enables the user to regain some of the depth of cut lost through the thickness of the template. This only applies, however, if the guidebush is of sufficient diameter to allow the collet to pass through it.

Most medium-power routers come equipped with a 17mm or 18mm guidebush as standard. This is too small to let the collet through, so we have to buy a larger bush. A 24mm bush will do nicely, indeed years ago the Elu 96 came with this

▲ Bosch GOF 900 ACE with a Trend sub-base, bush, a Titman long-reach cutter and centring tool

size. Then, for reasons best known to themselves, they changed it to 17mm. That's progress.

A word of warning. Trend guidebushes are fitted to most routers by means of two 5mm countersunk screws, but the DeWalt DW613 and the Power Devil have plain holes, which require nuts and bolts.

With the Trend T9 router the standard guidebushes are screwed to the inner plate by means of two 2BA screws, whose thread is nearly but not quite the same as 5mm. Check the screws before you fit the bush.

"A very useful feature is that the size is clearly marked on each bush"

▶ Unibase fitted to a Porter-Cable router with Trend guidebush and cutter fitted

Special sub-bases

Some routers, especially heavy-duty models, do not have a very good range of guide-bushes and do not take the Trend range. For most of these routers a false sub-base can be fitted to take the Trend and similar bushes.

There are two main such sub-bases, the Circular sub-base and the Unibase, both manufactured by Trend.

"The Unibase is a brand new product from Trend"

Circular sub-base

This is a 170mm diameter × 8mm thick piece of Tufnol, recessed to accept standard Trend guidebushes. It is drilled to suit the fixing points of the particular router for which it is ordered and the necessary fixings are supplied with the base.

Also supplied is an alignment kit so that the sub-base can be accurately centred on the cutter shank. Sub-bases are available for a very wide range of routers, ranging from the tiny Bosch POF 400 to the massive Ryobi RE 601.

The sub-base robs the user of 8mm depth of cut but with many guidebush applications this can be overcome by buying long-shank straight cutters. There are two ways of doing this.

The first way is to buy 'long-reach' cutters from Titman, or 'pocket' cutters from Trend. These have extra metal between the shank and the blades giving, as the name implies, longer reach.

The second method is to buy Leigh jig straight cutters, which have extra-long shanks to allow for the thickness of the Leigh jig dovetail comb. Most cutter suppliers include Leigh jig cutters in their range.

Unibase

The Unibase is a brand new product from Trend. It consists of an injection-moulded plastic disc, 170mm in diameter and 8mm thick which, like the Circular sub-base, is recessed to accept standard Trend guidebushes.

Unlike the Circular sub-base it is not specific to a particular router model. It has more holes than a colander, each of which is counter-bored to recess the top of a pan-head screw, and can be fitted to the base of most routers.

The recess will also take various other Trend-compatible guidebushes such as those supplied with the Leigh and Titan dovetail jigs. The Unibase is particularly useful for the many large routers that do not themselves boast a good range of guidebushes.

Examples include the Felisatti TP246E, Freud 2000, Makita 3612C, and Ryobi RE 601, but it is equally useful for some of the smaller models such as the Festo OF 1000E, Mafell LO50E and Makita 3620.

The Unibase comes complete with a plastic alignment bush and two pins to ensure concentricity of the cutter to the guidebush. The pins are stepped to fit ¼in, 8mm, 12mm and ½in collets. A packet of assorted fastenings completes the kit.

For routers with rather thick removable plastic sole plates, such as the Bosch 900 and 1300, Freud 2000, Ryobi RE601, the sole plate can be removed before fitting the Unibase to restore some of the lost depth of cut. Alternatively, long-reach straight cutters can be used for many jobs, as with the Circular sub-base.

▼ *The Unibase kit with centring pins, a dummy bush, nuts, bolts, washers and the Routing Wizard*

Routing free

A creative router doesn't have to be constrained with fences or jigs

FREEHAND routing, by which I mean routing without the aid of a side fence, bearing-guided cutter, straight edge, or any other form of assistance, is the best way to master your router.

It not only requires a steady hand and intense concentration, but also an understanding of how the rotation of the cutter exerts a force on the workpiece.

The force varies according to whether the cut is along, across, or diagonal to the grain. The appropriate counter-force must be applied to keep to the desired line of cut.

Freehand routing opens the door to many applications, such as sign making, relief carving and lettering. I shall begin

"Freehand routing opens the door to many applications"

by describing the basic freehand practice cuts that will develop confidence and control in your router handling (*see photo 1*).

Routers

You will, of course, use the particular

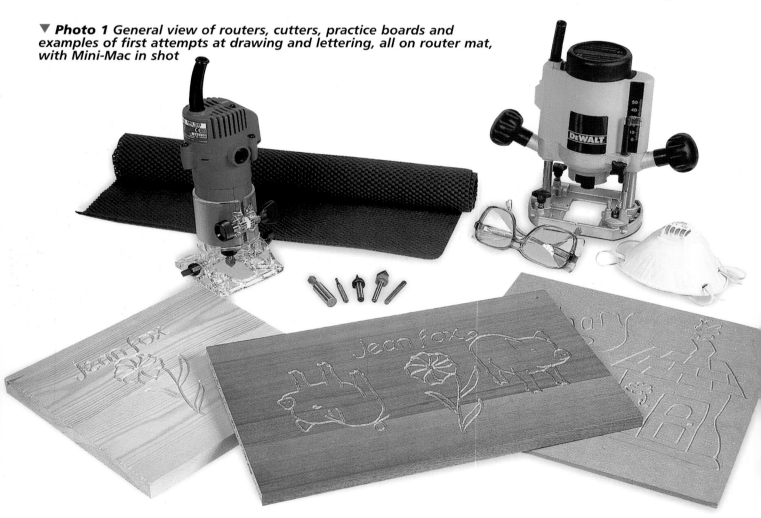

▼ **Photo 1** *General view of routers, cutters, practice boards and examples of first attempts at drawing and lettering, all on router mat, with Mini-Mac in shot*

"All freehand routing develops control"

router you happen to own, but the ideal machine for freehand work is a light-to-medium model with good visibility through the base plate and a simple, easily reached switch.

Good dust extraction is desirable, but with many routers the extractor spout effectively destroys visibility, and your freehand work will have to be done without it.

If you develop a taste for freehand routing and start to decorate box lids, draw pictures, or write names, you might well want to try a laminate trimming router. These are small lightweight models which also make excellent 'drawing instruments' because they can be used one-handed rather like a pencil or a brush.

The laminate trimmer shown is the Hitachi M6SB (*see photo 2*) but similar

▲ *Photo 3 Selection of cutters suitable for freehand work. Left to right: 2mm, 3mm, ¼in straight, Festo script, V- groover on ½in shank, CMT 'Laser', V-groover on ¼in shank, ¼in round-nose*

machines are available from DeWalt, Makita and others.

If your router does not fit the ideal profile this is no reason to avoid freehand routing. Admittedly, the big machines

such as the DeWalt 625, Freud 2000, or Trend T9, are not as easy to draw with as the Festo 1000, HolzHer 2356, or the Perles 808. The important thing is to practice doing it.

▼ *Photo 2 Selection of small and medium-duty routers suitable for freehand routing; Hitachi M6SB, DeWalt 613, Makita 3620, Trend T9*

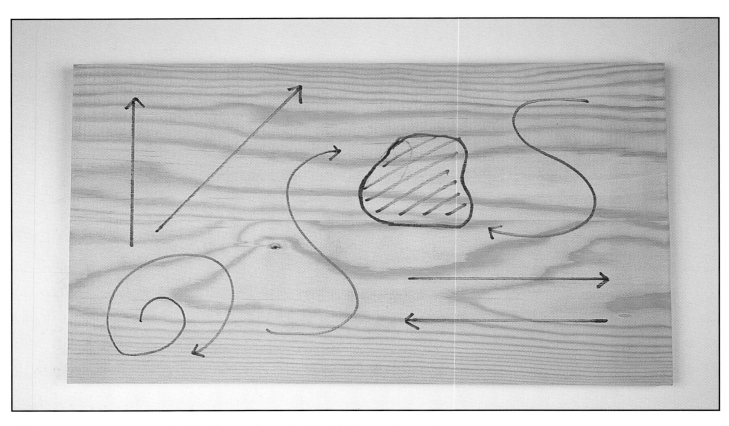

▲ **Photo 4** *Practice panel of softwood marked with lines of practice cuts*

▼ **Photo 5** *The Mini-Mac table in use*

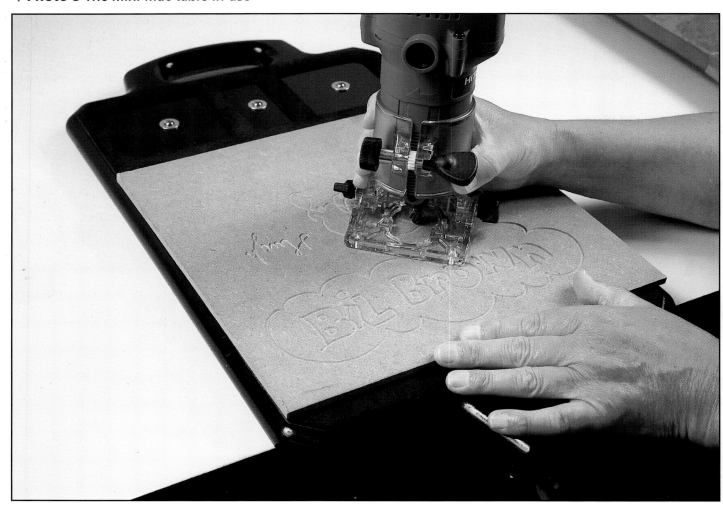

All freehand routing develops control; it doesn't matter if you never aspire to producing perfect copperplate house signs.

Cutters

Cutters should be narrow. Make first cuts with a straight cutter of not more than ¼in diameter, preferably less, in order to see clearly the path of your cut.

Further practice can be done with the V-grooving cutter included in most boxed sets, or you can buy more sophisticated cutters made specifically for veining, deep lettering and fine grooving.

These cutters widen the cut, making it more pronounced, by cutting a little deeper. To get you started however, the ¼in straight V-groover – and round-nose if you have one

"With freehand routing the router mat comes into its own"

– in your starter box of cutters will do nicely (*see photo 3*).

Material

Any timber or board material can be used for practice. This is one of the benefits of free-hand routing, since you can develop your skills on offcuts.

To start with I recommend a knot-free soft-wood board (*see photo 4*) as the distinct contrast between the hard and soft layers of grain will highlight the differences between cutting with, across, or diagonally through the grain.

Holding the workpiece

This depends partly on the shape and size of the practice piece, which can often be held directly in the jaws of a Workmate, or taped to the bench top.

With freehand routing the router mat comes into its own. With the mat spread on your bench top or suitable cutting table, the practice piece is simply laid on the mat, moved as necessary, and turned over when the first side has been routed.

▼ **Photo 6** *Making practice cuts. Note arms on worktable, workpiece well back from operator, additional light, and also safety goggles, facemask and ear defenders*

▲ *Photo 7 First attempts at freehand drawing*

This is all accomplished without the bother of clamps, which impede the progress of the router, or sticky tape, which can be messy and tedious to use.

The ultimate work-holding device for this type of work is the vacuum table, such as the Trend Mini-Mac (*see photo 5*). Nevertheless, the router mat runs the vacuum table to a close second.

Preparing the practice piece

Take several boards of softwood. On each of them draw a number of lines and curves with a marker pen or piece of chalk. Put an arrowhead on each line to denote the direction in which it is to be cut. Include an irregular shape and cross-hatch the interior (*see photo 4*).

The object of the exercise is to cut along the arrowed lines and inside the hatched shape. The target is to do this without any discernible deviation from the required line.

Working position

Since a steady hand and deep concentration are required, your working position must be comfortable and efficient. Work with your arms and elbows resting on the work surface or bench top, with the workpiece positioned well back from the front edge of your bench so you have to reach for it.

Small manipulations of the router are made by movements of the wrists and hands rather than the arms. You can, if you wish, sit down to the work. If you do, your seat should be the right height to allow your arms to stretch across the work surface.

Good light is important if you are following the lines on the practice piece, and an adjustable lamp is likely to prove useful.

You will be peering closely at your workpiece, so safety spectacles, a dust mask – since dust extraction is likely to prove impracticable – and ear defenders should all be worn (*see photo 6*).

Making the cuts

Set the cutter to a depth of about 2mm, plunge and lock the router, then position it with the base tilted so the cutter is clear of the workpiece, at the beginning of one of the lines.

Switch on, lower the cutter into the workpiece and slowly follow the line. Begin with one of the straight lines across the grain. The clockwise rotation of the cutter will tend to move the router to your left as you push it, and you will probably wander off the marked line.

Try a few more cuts and your ability to follow the line will improve. Make another cross-grain cut pulling the router. The rotation of the cutter will now try to take the router to your right as you pull it towards you.

Next, try the horizontal lines along the grain, cutting some from left to right and others from right to left. After that try the diagonal straight cuts and then the curves.

"By having to cut forwards, sideways, even backwards, you gain control of your router"

Finally, rout around the inside of the crosshatched figure, trying to keep just inside the boundary line. Do this with an anti-clockwise direction of cut the first time, then repeat in a clockwise direction.

While you are making these cuts think of the orthodox direction of cut with a router – against the rotation of the cutter and anti-clockwise around the outside of a figure – but be aware that you cannot always observe the orthodox wisdom.

It is no use, when halfway round the loop of a letter in your name, suddenly thinking, "Help. I'm going in the wrong direction". With freehand routing the rules go straight out of the window.

You move the router in the direction that draws the picture, or writes the letter. That is the great benefit of it. By having to cut forwards, sideways, even backwards, you gain control of your router.

Of course, you are working with narrow cutters at a very shallow depth of cut, so the force exerted by the rotation of the cutter is not so great that you will lose control of your cut. Nevertheless, you will certainly notice the difference between cuts across the grain,

"Don't be afraid of making a mess of your first efforts"

along the grain and diagonal to the grain.

You will undoubtedly err on the side of going too slow to begin with, and you will almost certainly experience burning somewhere along the way. With practice you will gradually speed up and the burning will disappear but, if it is persistent, reduce the depth of cut until you can make a comfortable, controlled, burn-free cut.

Having tried softwood, with its various grain formations, you can turn your hand to plywood, MDF or chipboard. The darker veneered chipboards are particularly rewarding because you can cut just deep enough to go through the veneer and reveal the contrast between the veneer and the underlying chipboard.

With the aid of the router mat or the vacuum table you can use up all manner of scrap pieces of timber and boards, even quite small ones. When you have mutilated one side you can simply turn the piece

over and tackle the other side.

Practice
Don't be afraid of making a mess of your first efforts – if it were easy we wouldn't have to practise it. Try different materials, and try varying the speed of the router if you have variable speed. Keep practising.

As you gain experience you will be able to follow more complicated curves, automatically compensating for the router's tendency to go its own way.

You will be able to make heavier cuts using larger cutters, and you will adapt your feed rates to the material being used. That is what the whole activity is aimed at – mastery of your router under different cutting conditions in different materials.

You can then try your hand, literally, at simple lettering and drawing. With a little practice you might be pleasantly surprised at your results (*see photos 7 and 8*).

▼ *Photo 8 Examples of freehand drawing and lettering showing what can be achieved after very little practice*

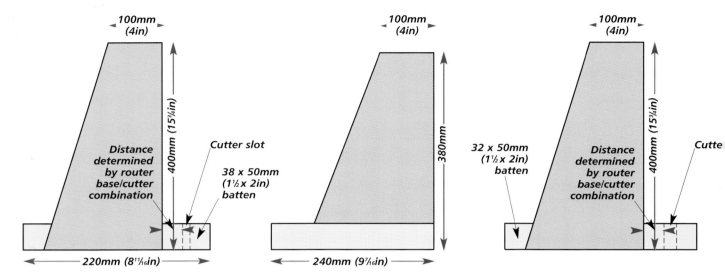

▲ Fig 1 Dimensions of cutting jig   **▲ Fig 2 Dimensions of trimming jig**   **▲ Fig 3 Dimensions of housing jig**

Fig 1: 100mm (4in); 400mm (15¾in); Distance determined by router base/cutter combination; Cutter slot; 38 x 50mm (1½ x 2in) batten; 220mm (8¹¹⁄₁₆in)

Fig 2: 100mm (4in); 380mm; 240mm (9⁷⁄₁₆in)

Fig 3: 100mm (4in); 32 x 50mm (1½ x 2in) batten; Distance determined by router base/cutter combination; 400mm (15¾in); Cutte[r]

THE router's reputation as the most versatile power tool in the workshop is usually attributed to the vast range of cutters available, although another reason is that many jobs are made possible by using simple home-made work aids that are easy to build.

False fence

This length of straight hardwood batten, fitted to the side fence of the router, provides a continuous unbroken run of fence and overcomes the 'run-in/run-out' problem at the beginning and end of a cut, for example when trenching.

Make the fence from mouldings available at DIY superstores. I use Burbidge's 10 × 20mm (⅜ × ¾in) stripwood.

Home help

Making and using simple work aids for hand routing

▲ Photo 1 Trend T9 fitted with false wooden fence, cutting trench in Contiboard

Cut a length about 450mm (17⅝in). Drill and countersink holes to take the machine screws or nuts and bolts for fixing to the router fence.

When rebating or working right on the edge of a panel, the cutter may plunge into the thickness of the false fence (*see photo 1*) requiring several fences to use with specific cutters.

Several of the most useful work aids are designed to be attached to the router base. First, make a pattern of your router base from which all future attachments can be made.

Making pattern

If your router has a detachable sole plate, remove it and tape it to a piece of 9mm MDF, placing two small pieces of hardboard or plywood between the sole plate and the MDF.

These should not obscure the fixing holes, or project outside the sole plate. Their purpose is to separate the two workpieces so the bearing of a flush-trimming cutter can run on the sole plate without cutting into it.

Rough-cut around the MDF and drill the fixing holes, using the holes in the sole plate as your template. Trim the MDF flush with

"Several of the most useful work aids are designed to be attached to the router base"

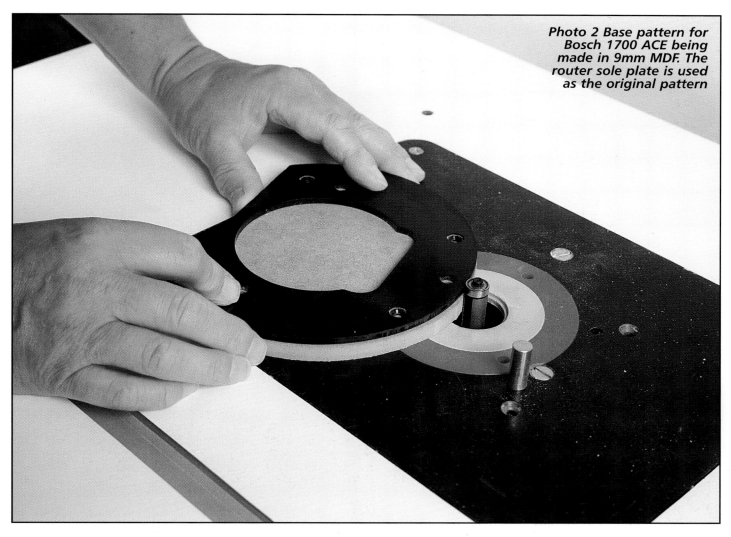

the sole plate, using the router – minus sole plate – in a table, and the flush-trimming cutter (*see photo 2*).

To get some leeway with the hole positioning, use a twist drill very slightly larger than the required holes. Many routers have two or three 6mm tapped holes in their base for fixing purposes. If you use a ¼in twist drill you'll give yourself a 0.35mm margin on each hole.

In the absence of a router table, the pattern can be finished by drawing round the router sole plate, removing it from the MDF, and cutting or sanding the MDF to shape. The hardboard spacing pieces are not needed here.

If your router sole plate is not detachable, make a paper rubbing of the base, or drill holes in a piece of 9mm MDF to fix to the router, draw round the base, and cut or sand to shape as above (*see photo 3*).

If your router has only guidebush holes, use a guidebush as a template for the attachment holes.

▼ *Photo 3 A selection of MDF base patterns, all labelled*

▼ *Photo 4 T5 and Bosch 900 ACE fitted with anti-tilt plates*

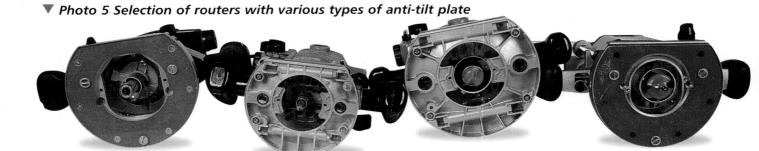

False bases

Armed with your base pattern you can make a range of false bases. While they can be made from MDF or plywood, for many purposes Perspex, or one of the other transparent 'window plastics' is better.

Make bases with different-size apertures to suit different diameter cutters for edge-moulding, flush trimming, housings and drilling.

Many DIY shops have a stock of offcuts of plastic glass substitutes big enough for router bases.

Drilling base

The drilling base fitted to the Hitachi M8V is also of note. The router makes an excellent drill, especially when used on large panels where the required holes are too far from the edge to fit under the throat of a drill stand, cutting a clean hole at a perfect right-angle and at a precisely controlled depth.

"Many routers have two or three 6mm tapped holes in their base for fixing purposes"

The M8V drilling base was made to drill a number of ⅜in holes. Having cut the basic shape and countersunk the attachment holes, I screwed the plate to the router base and plunged the router, with a V-grooving cutter in the collet – router unplugged – to the surface of the false base.

This gave me a dot in the dead centre of the base through which I scratched the two cross-hair lines to position the router, rubbing them with black paint to make them show.

"One of the best ways to prevent tilting when hand routing the edge of a panel is to fit a base extension made of MDF, plywood or Perspex to your router"

▼ *Photo 6 Three simple jigs for cutting, trimming and housing*

Photo 7 Cutting jig in use on Contiboard, with HolzHer 2356 router and ¼in cutter

As I wanted to drill ⅜in holes, I plunged a ½in straight cutter through the false base to give me a dead-centre hole with clearance.

Anti-tilt plates

One of the best ways to prevent tilting when hand routing the edge of a panel is to fit a

base extension made of MDF, plywood or Perspex to your router. With one hand, press the extension handle to the work surface, using the other hand to propel the router around the edge of the panel (*see photo 4*). Small and medium routers like the Bosch 900 ACE and the Trend T5 are particularly suitable.

Big heavy routers are less suitable;.for these a larger base extension fitted with two handles works best.

The anti-tilt plate is made from 9mm or 12mm MDF, depending on how deep you can plunge your router. Use the base pattern to position the fixing holes and get the shape of the anti-tilt plate right.

I cover both sides with plastic laminate, but this is not essential. Make the centre hole with the hole saw as for transparent bases.

The anti-tilt plates shown on the big Hitachi, Trend and DeWalt models are particularly useful for heavy-duty routers with large base apertures (*see photo 5*).

You can make several, cutting the central hole as required. I use an old set of cheap Japanese hole saws to cut the central holes in the bases.

The hole-saws are carried on a ¼in drill, so I attach the false base to the router, fit a ¼in straight cutter and plunge it through the base to give me a dead-centre hole to locate the appropriate size of hole saw.

"I just get on with it and think positively"

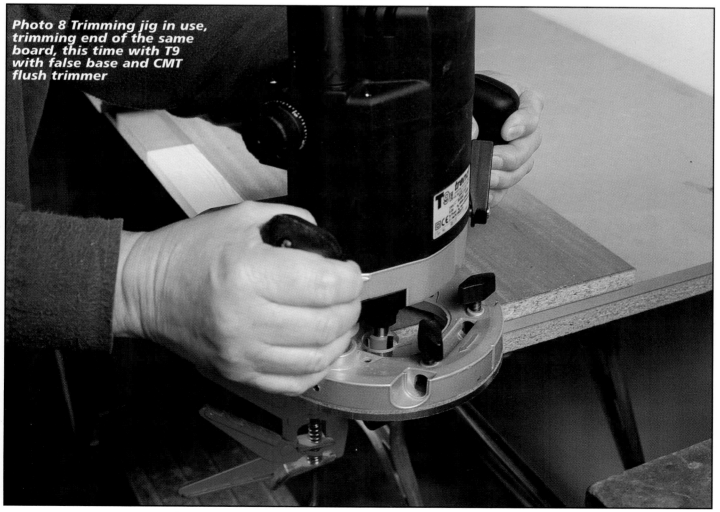

Photo 8 Trimming jig in use, trimming end of the same board, this time with T9 with false base and CMT flush trimmer

Carpentry aids

These three simple jigs are among the most often used in my workshop (*see photo 6*).

They let the user cut, trim and house boards using only simple cutters, and are particularly suitable for ready-made boards of standard widths, such as veneered chipboard.

They are made of pieces of 9mm or 12mm MDF or plywood with lengths of batten glued to them. The edges of the MDF and the batten are machined absolutely straight and glued together at right angles, rather like the T-square used with a portable circular saw.

I use a straightforward rubbed joint with PVA glue. This is frowned on by purists, but I have never had one of these joints come apart.

Resist the temptation to make them large enough to cater for a massive board, or you will be constantly struggling with them on the more common board widths.

Cutting jig

Glue a fairly thick piece of batten 38 × 50mm (1½ × 2in) nominal to the MDF with a simple rubbed joint, and set at right angles with a square. Reserve the jig for a particular diameter cutter and mark accordingly.

Start by making a test cut in a piece of board, letting the cutter cut its own groove through the batten.

If the jig is reserved for that one cutter, the groove acts as an automatic registration mark for positioning the cut (*see fig 1*).

This overcomes the problem of allowing for the distance from the edge of the cutter to the edge of the router base, when positioning your straight edge.

The thick batten enables panels of common thickness, 15 or 18mm (⅝ or ¾in), to be cut without cutting right through the batten, preserving the length of the straight edge (*see photo 7*).

Trimming jig

This trimming jig is very useful for trimming softwood boards to exact length, and leaving a polished finish across the end grain.

You'll need a thin piece of batten, 16mm (⅝in) or less. Glue this to the MDF, with the end of the batten flush with the edge of the MDF (*see fig 2*).

The jig is used with a bearing-guided panel-trim cutter. Rough-cut the workpiece, and trim it to the exact length by registering the pencil line against the end of the batten.

The trimming cut brings the board precisely to length with an exact right angle, both across the width and in the thickness.

It is as accurate as the cutting jig, and considerably quicker if a batch of boards is being prepared (*see photo 8*).

The batten must be thin, as it must not exceed the thickness of the panel being trimmed. Unlike the cutting jig, the trimming jig is not specific to a particular router/cutter combination.

Housing jig

This is like the cutting jig, but made with a medium thickness 32 × 50mm (1¼ × 2in) nominal batten – since housings do not go right through the panel – and is reserved for a larger-diameter cutter.

I call this my 'poor man's housing jig'. It is used with a cutter very slightly smaller in diameter than the thickness of the board to be housed, so you take a cut marginally too narrow for the housing and move the jig to widen it.

Take your first cut very carefully, so as not to over-widen the housing. By the time you have made the second one your eye will be in, and you'll be shifting the jig just the right amount (*see photo 9*).

For stopped housings, tape a piece of MDF or other board to the jig in the appropriate position.

Some people worry about spoiling the cut by letting the router base wander away from the edge of the jig. I just get on with it and think positively.

Photo 9 Housing jig in use with Perles OF 808 router and ⅝in Wealden cutter

Moulding the edge of a softwood block

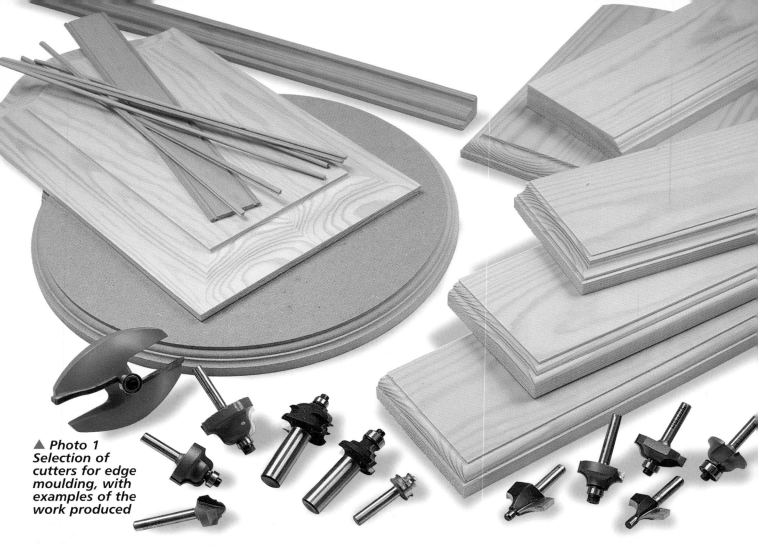

On the edge

Advice for beginners on routing perfect edges and mouldings

DECORATIVE edges and mouldings are the trademark of the router. There is a vast range of cutters available, enabling attractive edges to be applied to table tops, door panels, box lids and bases. With the router held in the hand, edges can be moulded with plain, pin-guided or bearing-guided cutters (*see photo 1*).

Plain cutters have no integral guiding device and should be used in conjunction with a side fence, roller follower or router table with a fence. Guided cutters have a built-in guiding device that can mean quicker setting up and easier use, but they have restrictions as the position of the cut is fixed.

Side fence

Plain cutters are usually used with the router side fence for putting a moulding along the edge of a straight workpiece (*see photo 2*).

The most common problem in using the router side fence is that of run-in/run-out, where the entry and exit points of the cut are difficult to control.

Fitting a false wooden fence to your router side fence gives a longer, steadier guide for the beginning and end of the cut. The false fence should be thick enough to accommodate part of the circumference of the cutter when working a very narrow edge.

"Fitting a false wooden fence to your router side fence gives a longer, steadier guide for the beginning and end of the cut"

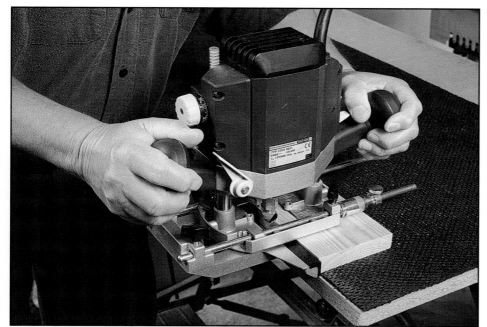

Roller follower

For curved work, with a plain cutter, a roller follower is sometimes provided by the router manufacturer (*see photo 3*). Sometimes called an edge follower, a roller follower consists of a horizontally-mounted wheel fitted to the normal side fence or to a fence bracket. Its purpose is to run against the edge of a curved workpiece, to guide the cutter, and can also be run against the edge of a pattern fastened below a workpiece, to reproduce the shape.

Roller followers can be difficult to use successfully. If the router is pivoted on the roller, the cutter moves in an arc, possibly producing an inconsistent moulding on the edge of the workpiece.

The axis of the wheel and cutter must be aligned at right angles to the edge of the workpiece to produce a good result, but even with practice results are rather hit and miss. In addition, some followers, including the Elu model shown, have a metal wheel which can easily mark the edge of the workpiece. I try to avoid the roller follower at all costs, using a bearing-guided cutter instead.

For circular workpieces a trammel bar can be used with a plain cutter for edge moulding.

▲ **Photo 2 Example of an edge moulded with a plain cutter and router side fence**

▼ **Photo 3 Same cutter used with a roller follower to mould the edge of a circular plaque**

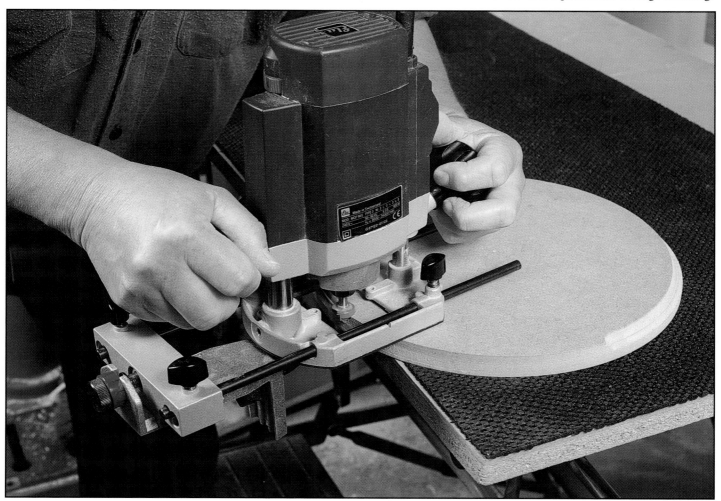

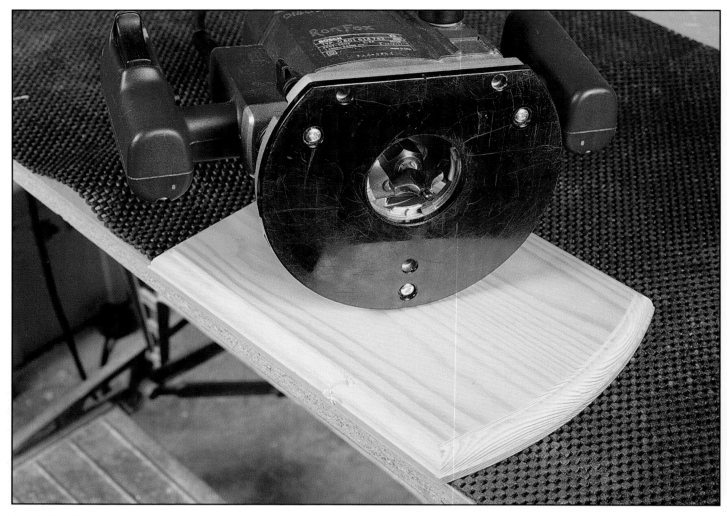

Guided cutters

Guided cutters fall into two types, pin-guided and bearing-guided.

Pin-guided cutters have a small pin formed into the end of the cutter. The pin is run against the edge of the workpiece and, being part of the cutter, rotates at cutter speed. It is thus very easy to burn both the edge of the work and the pin if you are heavy-handed. Apart from this drawback, however, the pin-guided cutter can get closer into corners and follow a more intricate pattern than the bearing-guided version (*see photo 4*).

Bearing-guided cutters are commonly used for applying edge mouldings (*see photo 5*). The bearing controls the width of the cut and rolls along the edge of the workpiece at a rotation speed determined by the rate of feed of the router, so the possibility of burning is reduced.

"I try to avoid the roller follower at all costs, using a bearing-guided cutter instead"

▲ *Photo 4 Ovolo mould applied to the edge of a small panel with a pin-guided cutter*

▼ *Photo 5 Blocks for storing router cutters etc., moulded with a Roman ogee and ovolo cutters*

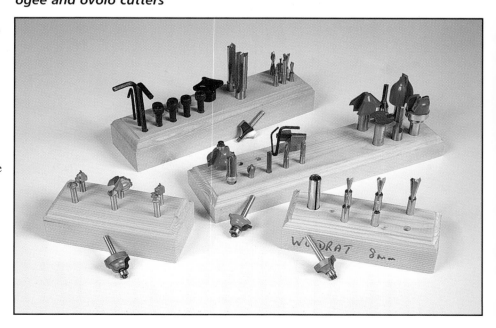

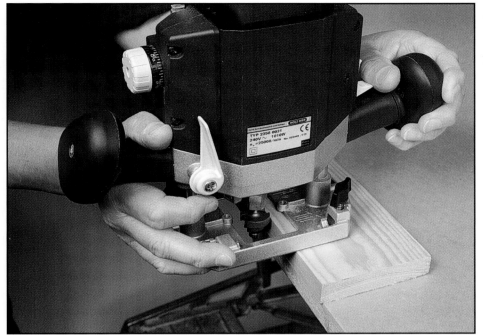

▲ *Photo 6 Bearing-guided cutter being set to full depth by eye*

▼ *Photo 7 Selection of routers with various types of anti-tilt plate*

Cutting mouldings

For good results, the edge of the work-piece must be absolutely smooth and square, as any irregularity or ripple will be faithfully followed by the pin or bearing, although this can be reduced by using a side fence.

Holding the workpiece can be the most difficult part of the job, and I find that for much hand-held edge moulding the router mat comes into its own.

> **"The edge of the workpiece must be absolutely smooth and square as any irregularity or ripple will be faithfully followed by the pin or bearing"**

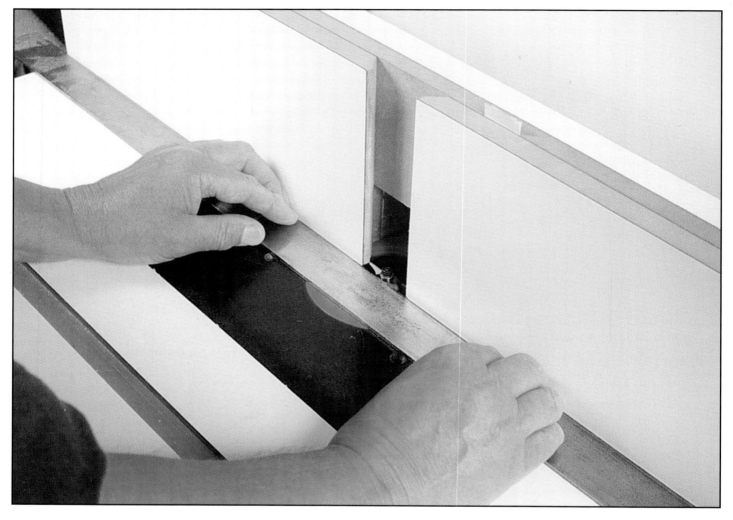

When using a plain cutter the edge of the side fence or roller follower is usually aligned with the centre line of the cutter. The width of the cut can be varied by adjusting this setting. With a pin- or bearing-guided cutter the pin or bearing determines the width of the cut, but note that with a bearing-guided cutter, fitting different diameter bearings can vary the width and shape of the cut.

The moulding should always be cut in a series of light passes, taking a very light final pass for the best possible finish. The shape of the cutter helps determine the depth of each pass.

Begin with an end grain and work anti-clockwise around the outside of a figure and clockwise around the inside.

Keep moving steadily across end grain to avoid burning the wood, but if burning does occur, try removing it with a careful 'wrong-direction' cut.

Note that you cannot plunge a cutter that has a pin or a bearing's Allen screw at its centre. The depth of cut is therefore set by eye to its full depth and the cut taken in easy stages towards this final depth (*see photo 6*).

If an exact match to an existing moulding

▲ *Photo 8 Bearing-guided cutter being aligned with table fence using a straight edge*

is required, a test piece will be necessary. To achieve the precise final depth of cut, use the fine height adjuster – if your router has one.

An effective way of making fine adjustments is to hook the right thumb over the handle and 'squeeze' the router, with it switched off of course.

Note also that with many moulding cutters an attractive edge can be obtained without going to the full depth of the cutter. For example, the Roman ogee gives a pleasant cove-like edge to lids and bases of small boxes by simply using the lower curve of the cutter.

Table versus hand

I favour carrying out edge moulding on a router table rather than by hand-held router, size of workpiece depending, because the cut is much less stressful, so more likely to be accurate, the run-in/run-out problem does not arise and tilting is less likely.

The cut is 'fail-safe' in that if it kicks up from the table or away from the fence there is no over-cut and the workpiece merely has to be passed over the cutter again.

Because many of the heavier cutters can only be used in a stationary router, the table extends your scope.

Ideally your router should be a variable speed model so that the speed can be set according to the diameter of the cutter. A special case of a large cutter for edge moulding is the making of raised panels for doors (see photos 1 and 10).

Tilt

No matter how wide your panel, only half the router base is on the workpiece when you are moulding the edge.

The simplest way to overcome this tilt problem, if the workpiece allows, is to place a board of equal thickness to the workpiece parallel to the side being routed, thus forming a 'bridge' to support the router base.

The idea can be extended to fit a 'shoe' of the appropriate thickness to the outer edge of the router base to keep the router level. A more versatile version of the shoe is Bob Wearing's adjustable levelling foot.

The most common method of overcoming tilt, however, is to fit a false base or base extension to the router, *see photo 7*. With heavy-duty routers with large base apertures, make a false base of transparent plastic, cutting a hole to provide minimum clearance for the cutter.

Table routing

Think of the table as a gigantic upended router. The tabletop is the router base, the table fence takes the place of the router side-fence and the fine adjuster or plunge-bar is used to set the height – meaning depth – of cut.

With this analogy in mind it is easy to see that moulding the edge of a board by passing it over a cutter against the fence is an exact upside-down version of hand-routing techniques.

As with hand-held routing, mouldings can be cut with plain, pin-guided or bearing-guided cutters. With plain cutters the table fence is set to control the width of cut. Fine adjustment is made by pivoting the fence on one of its fastening bolts.

If a bearing-guided cutter is to be used for a straight cut with the table fence, the bearing is left on the cutter and the fence aligned with the front of the bearing, *see photo 8*.

For curved work the table fence is removed and the cut made with a bearing-guided or pin-guided cutter.

With most router tables, removing the fence automatically removes the guards and dust extraction, so I use a simple home-made device that combines the two functions.

Also necessary is some kind of lead-in guide to overcome the need to push the workpiece straight into the cutter – I use a pin but an alternative is a shaped batten.

For the set-up for moulding a curved edge with the fence removed, *see photo 9*, note the home-made guard/dust port and the lead-in pin.

If possible the cut is taken in several light passes, just as in hand-held routing. Because of the difficulty of setting depth of cut, this operation is not easy, resulting in a regrettable but understandable tendency to set the height of cut to the full and make the cut in one pass. A long-overdue solution comes with the introduction of WoodRat Universal Plungebars that can be fitted to most routers and make the job of depth setting easier.

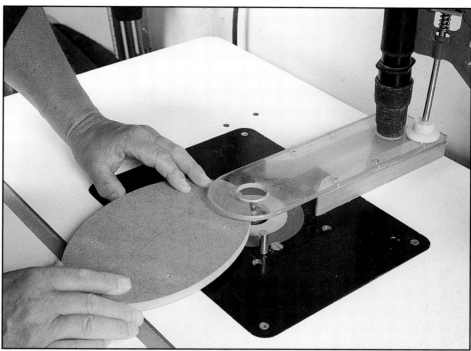

▲ *Photo 9 Set-up for moulding with table fence removed. Note home-made guard/dust port and lead-in pin*

"An effective way of making fine adjustments is to hook the right thumb over the handle and 'squeeze' the router"

▼ *Photo 10 Panel raising in progress with a horizontal panel-raising cutter*

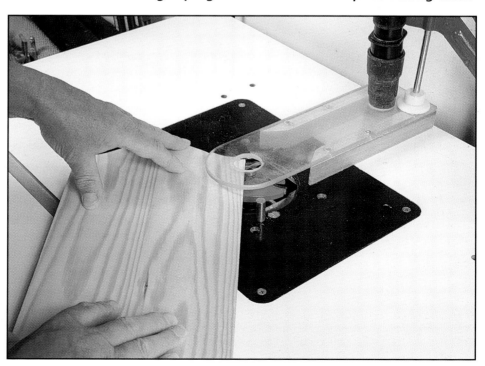

Routing a round

Getting to grips with cutting curves

THE router is excellent for cutting clean, accurate curves and circles. The principle is simple. Fasten a bar or board to the base of the router, and set a pivot pin at the required radius. Use the router like a compass and pencil, making several passes if neccessary.

Trammel bars

A selection of circle-cutting devices, most of them home-made, are shown in *photo 1*. Many routers come with a circle-cutting device, or have one as an accessory.

Some, like the Bosch 500/600, involve screwing a pin to the router side fence, giving a limited range of radii. Fitting a pivot pin to one of the side-fence rods is better.

Makes include the Perles OF808, Trend T5, Trend T9, or the trammel bar as offered for the Elu/ DeWalt range (*see photo 1*) included in the DeWalt DE 6900 Accessory Kit and available separately under part number DE 6905.

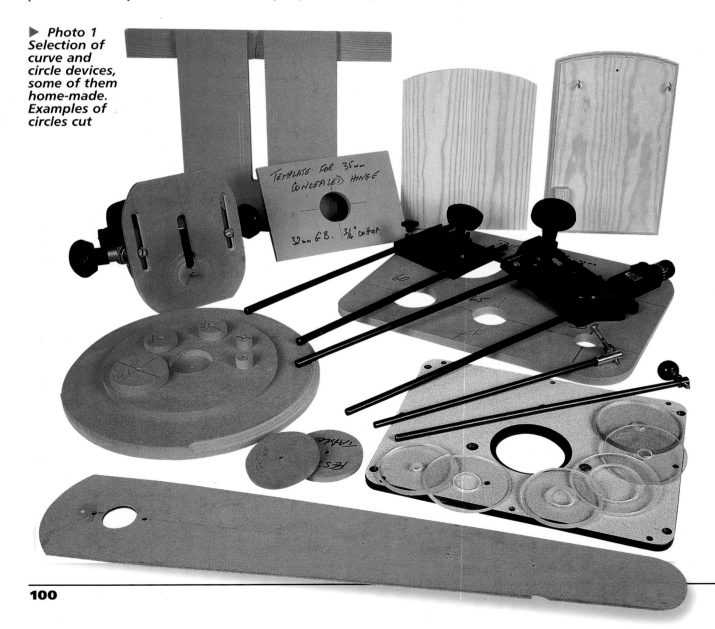

▶ *Photo 1 Selection of curve and circle devices, some of them home-made. Examples of circles cut*

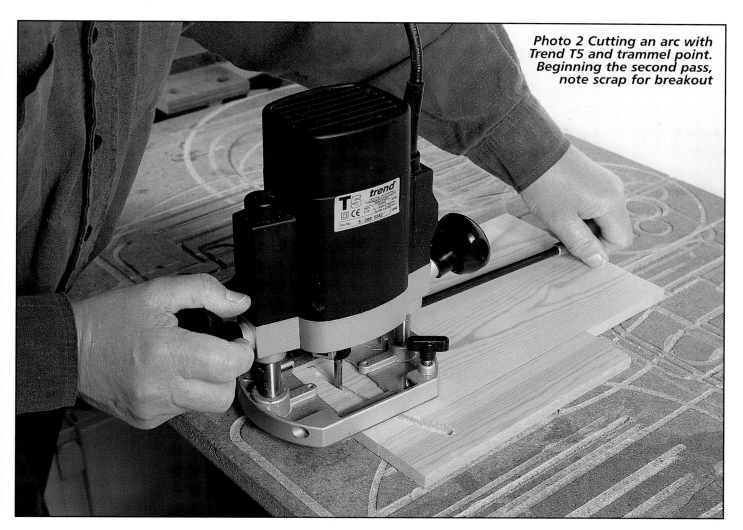

Trammel bars are easy to use. Put the bar in the router in one of the fence-rod positions. The pivot end consists of a sharpened pin, which might need a hole drilled for it at the centre of the circle. Some pins are sharp, and simply push into the workpiece.

Mark the point of origin on the workpiece, setting the radius by sliding the trammel bar and tightening the thumbscrew. Drop the pin into the drilled hole – or push it into the workpiece – and with the router set for the initial cut, swing across the panel.

The maximum radius is determined by the rod length. Longer rod lengths should be obtainable from your local metal stockist.

Cutting curves

A small curved panel is shown being cut in *photo 2*. Hold the panel to the cutting table with double-sided tape. Place some tape under the line of cut to stop the off-cut flying loose, and spoiling the cut.

Release the plunge at the end of each pass, return the router to the starting position, and plunge for the next cut. Repeat until the cut is complete.

As this cut goes right through the workpiece, make the final cut by switching on the router before plunging the cutter to the full cutting depth.

After the final cut, the tip of the cutter may be coated with tape adhesive. Remove with cutter-cleaning solvent before cutting again. A simple process, but there are several points to note:–

1. Fasten pieces of scrap material the same thickness as the workpiece to both sides of the cut. These support the router on the input side, and prevent breakout on the output side.

2. The correct direction of cut is not always obvious. Remember, 'anti-clockwise around the outside of a figure, clockwise around the inside'.

The panel is being made in *photo 2*, so I

Photo 3 A two-rod trammel steadies the Bosch 1300 router; 4 mm hole drilled for pivot pin

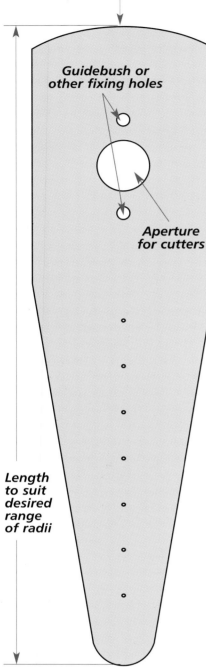

Shape to fit base of router

Guidebush or other fixing holes

Aperture for cutters

Length to suit desired range of radii

▲ Fig 1 Dimensions of home-made trammel bar

▲ *Photo 4 A shallow curve being cut with a home-made trammel bar.Note radius longer than panel so length of same-thickness wood is placed to take bradawl as pivot pin*

▼ *Photo 5 Cutting a complete circle with a two-rod trammel bar, DeWalt 625E, De 6285 base plate extension and fence rods as trammel. Left hand on pivot knob, right hand on router handle. Hands about to change over*

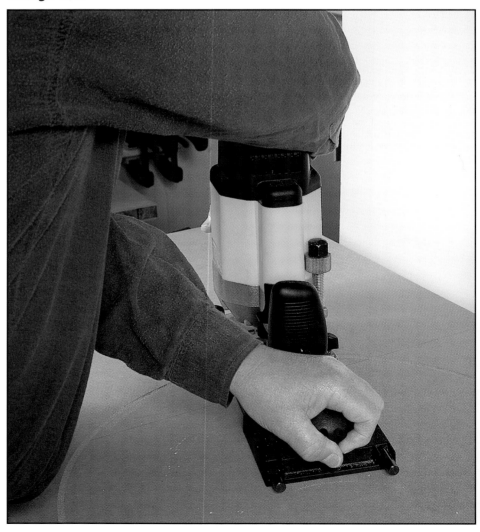

am cutting anti-clockwise, from left to right in the photograph.

Had I been making a hole in the front of a loudspeaker cabinet, the hole would have been the 'product', and the circular disc the waste. Here I would cut in a clockwise direction.

3. A single trammel bar pivoting on a pin isn't very stable, as it's easy to lift the pin out of the panel or tilt the router. Sharp pins can 'stretch' the centre hole, especially in softwood, losing accuracy and spoiling the edge of the cut.

4. You may not want to mark the surface of your workpiece with the pivot pin.

◀ *Photo 6 Guidebush guide used with HolzHer 2356 cutting counter slots for small circle cutter*

"It helps if some tape is placed under the line of the cut"

Often it won't matter if the workpiece is marked by a pin hole or a drilled hole. For example, a circular table top can be cut face down, and might end up with a socket or under-frame concealing the original hole.

Home-made

An alternative to a commercial trammel fitting is a home-made one of plywood, MDF or Perspex. Screw a suitable length of material to the router base, with a hole for the cutter to plunge through.

Make a hole for the pivot pin the required distance from the cutter. The trammel pivots on a pin driven into the workpiece, or a thin hand-held bradawl.

Instead, you could make two short counter-slotted cuts for fastening to the router. This allows you to make fine adjustments to the radius of the cut if the centre-hole is drilled slightly out.

The board width in this kind of trammel gives the same 'anti-tilt' properties as the twin-bar commercial trammel.

The dimensions of a typical MDF trammel bar I made for my Elu 96 are shown in *fig 1*. It also fits the DeWalt 613, the Perles OF808, the Trend T5, the HolzHer 2356 and several other routers.

To cut a shallow curve in a small panel, the trammel is used with a bradawl as the pivot (*see photo 4*). Here the radius is longer than the length of the workpiece, so a piece of wood the same thickness as the panel is clamped or taped to the cutting table. The trammel will run smoothly without tilt.

For larger curves, such as dining tables, it's common to make a one-off trammel from a length of board and discard it upon completion.

Circles

Cutting a circle is straightforward, but tends to deter beginners. Swing the router on its pivot point until your arms are crossed, then change hands to complete the cut.

It helps if you support the power cable from the workshop ceiling. I cut a 450mm disc in MDF, using a two-rod trammel with the DeWalt 625E (*see photo 5*).

The trammel consists of the side-fence

"Anti-clockwise around the outside of a figure, clockwise around the inside"

A two-bar trammel is much steadier than a single bar. Many router manufacturers offer a plastic base plate, often as part of another accessory. This converts the fence rods to a two-bar trammel.

The Bosch version, used with the GOF 1300 ACE router, is illustrated in *photo 3*. The plastic plate is the circle guide and guide rail adapter with fine adjuster – Part No. 2 609 200 143.

The twin bars and the hefty knob on top transform the cutting process, the whole set-up becoming much more stable.

All these devices work with existing router fence rods, many of which are interchangeable between makes and models. The DeWalt DE 6905 trammel bar fits any router with 8mm fence rods, and the Bosch plastic base fits the fence rods of most medium-power routers (*see photo 3*).

Avoid making holes and marks in the workpiece by taping a piece of 6mm plywood or MDF to it. Drill this to take the pivot pin. To keep the trammel parallel to the work surface, screw or tape a piece of material the same thickness to your router base.

▼ *Photo 7 The finished slots with jig and router*

"The twin bars and hefty knob on top transform the cutting process"

▲ *Photo 8 Small circle-cutting jig with radius being set with the aid of a vernier gauge*

▲ *Photo 9 The small circle cutter in use. A circle part cut through a board*

rods mounted on the DE 6285 base plate extension. My left hand is on the trammel knob, and right hand on the router handle. I have pivoted the router anti-clockwise as far as is comfortable.

I am about to move my right hand from the router handle to the pivot knob, transferring my left hand from the pivot knob to the router handle.

Remember to keep hold of the pivot knob with the left hand until the right hand is ready to take over. It's not quite as hair-raising as it sounds!

The trouble with trammel bars is that the smallest cutting radius is determined by the router base size, and often you want to cut very small circles.

A home-made small circle jig is invaluable here. First you must make another simple work aid. I call this my 'guidebush guide', and made it for cutting counter-slots in jigs like the small circle cutter.

Guidebush guide

The guidebush guide is a piece of MDF with a slot cut in it, giving a snug fit to a guidebush. It enables straight cuts to be made with a guidebush fitted. The MDF and slot length can be any size.

If different diameter cutters are used without moving the jig, each successive cut is laid over the previous ones. This enables you to counter-slot the board.

Make a through cut with a narrow cutter, giving clearance to the shank of the bolt, then a shallow cut with a wider cutter to make a recess for the bolt head.

"It's not quite as hair-raising as it sounds!"

The guidebush size isn't important, but must accept the largest diameter cutter you want to use. Glue a length of 32 × 50mm (1× 1¼in) batten to the open edge of the MDF, at right angles to the slot.

The dimensions of one I made for a 24mm guidebush are shown in *fig 2*. This is seen fitted to the HolzHer 2356 (*see photo 6*).

Although made for counter-slotting, the guidebush guide is a good alternative to the housing jig (*see page 98*), because the guidebush running in the slot stops the router deviating from the cut.

Small circle jig

Using the guidebush guide, make the small circle jig by slotting and counter-slotting a piece of MDF or Perspex, shaping it to fit the base of your router, and drilling the hole for the pivot pin.

The spacing of the attachment holes and jig shape are both derived from the MDF pattern of your router base (*see page 88*).

The dimensions of one I made for my Elu 96E are shown in *fig 3*. It fits a number of other models with similar spaced attachment holes, and the idea can be applied to other makes and models.

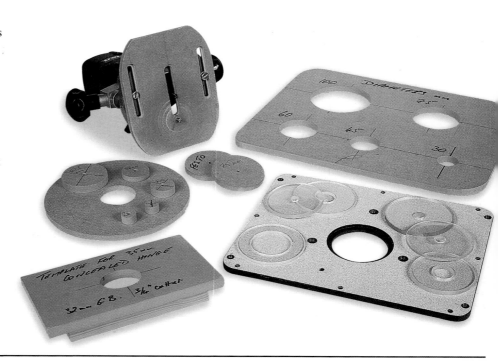

The material should be at least 9mm thick, to take the counter-slots that recess the heads of the attachment screws. Cut three slots in the underside of the plate.

Two are spaced apart the distance of your router-base attachment points, and counter-slotted to let you screw the plate to the base without the screw heads standing proud of the plate. The third slot allows the cutter to plunge through. A width of ½in should do for most work.

"Push the pin into the hole, switch on the router and plunge"

Insert a short pin of suitable diameter into a hole drilled near the end of the cutter slot. Set it in epoxy resin glue for added strength. I used 6mm silver steel rod for my pivot pin.

Set the radius of the cut using the recessed screws and a vernier gauge (*see photo 8*).

Remember the centre of the circle is the centre of the pivot pin. By using a convenient diameter pin – in this case 6mm – you can subtract the pin radius from the circle radius and measure from the edge of the pin.

The setting depends on whether you are cutting the hole or the disc. In the first case the radius is measured to the outer cutter blade, in the second, to the inner cutter blade.

With the radius set, drill a hole for the pivot pin in the workpiece. Use a scrap piece, if you don't want to drill holes in the workpiece. Push the pin into the hole, switch on the router and plunge. Take the first pass in an anti-clockwise direction and make successive shallow passes until the cut is complete.

The small circle cutter is shown fitted to the Trend T5 router, with a half-completed cut in a piece of MDF in *photo 9*.

Commercial jigs

This is one of the easiest router cuts to make. The router sits firmly on the workpiece, and pivots without any suggestion that it will come out of the cut. Hand positions can be changed without fear of spoiling the cut.

The small circle cutter is shown fitted to the router, with a selection of circles cut with it, including the hole in the router table top in *photo 10*.

Commercial jigs for cutting circles and ellipses, notably the Trend Mini Ellipse and Circle Cutting Jig, and the Pivot Frame Jig, go beyond the simple devices described above.

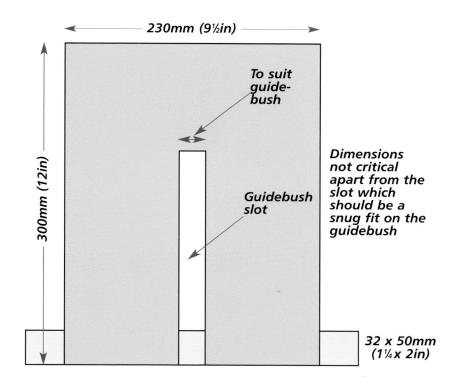

◄ Fig 2 Dimensions of guidebush guide

230mm (9½in)

300mm (12in)

To suit guide-bush

Guidebush slot

Dimensions not critical apart from the slot which should be a snug fit on the guidebush

32 x 50mm (1¼x 2in)

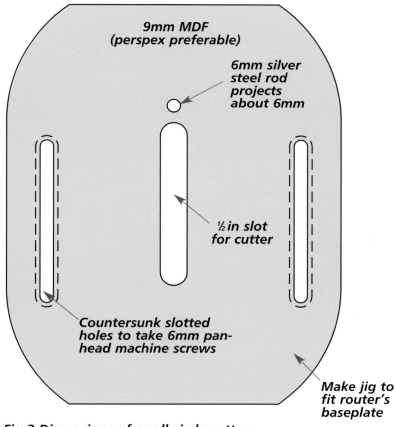

◄ Fig 3 Dimensions of small circle cutter

9mm MDF (perspex preferable)

6mm silver steel rod projects about 6mm

½in slot for cutter

Countersunk slotted holes to take 6mm pan-head machine screws

Make jig to fit router's baseplate

Working to a
pattern

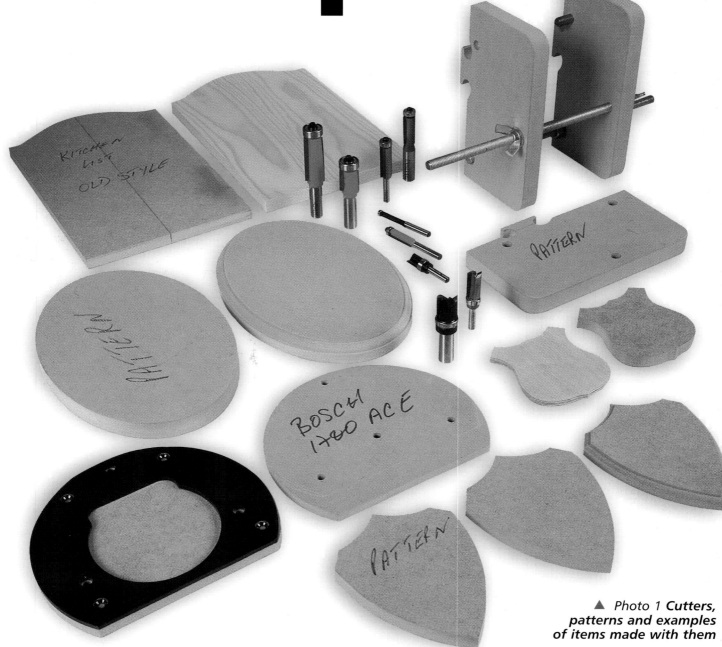

▲ *Photo 1 **Cutters,
patterns and examples
of items made with them***

ALL router users are faced from time
to time with the need to produce a
number of identical items, be they
plaques, shields, photo frames,
parts for toys or whatever.

One of the most productive ways of doing
this is to make an original. This pattern can

then be used to replicate as many copies as
are needed, using the router in a table with a
flush-trimming cutter – with the bearing on
the end – or a profile-guide cutter – with the
bearing above the cutting edges (*see photo 1*).

The method is not confined to batch
production. Frequently, a single copy of a

particular item is called for. A good example
is a pattern for the base of your router, using
the router's own plastic sole plate as the
original (*see page 110*).

Pattern routing can be illustrated with the
making of a small trophy shield. The
original is drawn onto a piece of plywood or

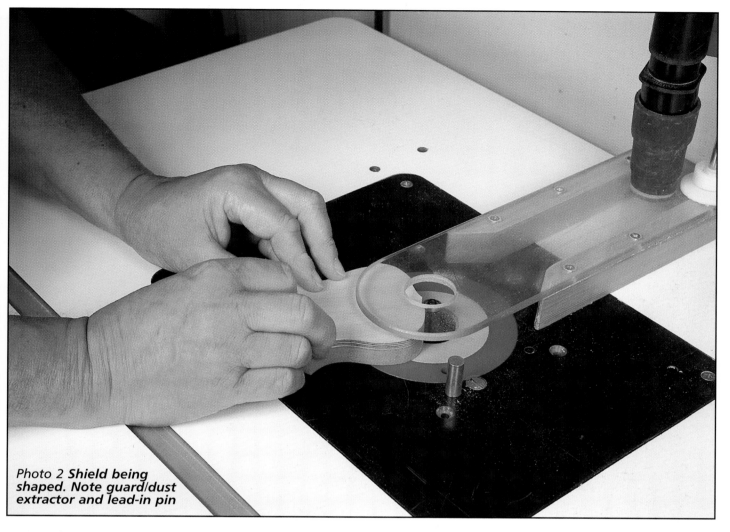

Photo 2 **Shield being shaped. Note guard/dust extractor and lead-in pin**

Photo 3 **Separating pattern and workpiece with marking knife**

MDF; alternatively the design is drawn on to a sheet of paper and stuck to the surface of the material with photographic spray mount.

The shield is then cut out with a fretsaw or coping saw and shaped with a rasp, file or sanding bobbin.

Because the bearing-guided cutters will follow the edge of the pattern exactly, reproducing every ridge and ripple, it is crucial to achieve a perfect pattern from which to make copies.

Next, draw around the master pattern on the workpiece and rough-cut to shape, trying to leave a border of no more than 3mm (⅛in).

The pattern is then attached to the workpiece with double-sided heavy carpet tape bought from a DIY superstore.

Two small pieces of tape are pressed onto the pattern and the pattern is placed lightly on the workpiece, the reason for this being that the hardest part of the job is usually separating the pattern and workpiece after the cut is completed.

Applying only light pressure with the first few pieces makes it possible to separate pattern and workpiece while leaving the tape on the pattern, ready to use for the next cut. I reckon to achieve between six and 12 workpieces from each application of the tape.

"Rotating in a clockwise direction is likely to result – with dire consequences – in the workpiece being whipped out of our hands"

Table set-up

The cut can be made with either a top- or a bottom-bearing cutter. I prefer the bottom-mounted type for this particular job because, with the router inverted in the table, the bearing is uppermost and the pattern is on top, with the hands holding the workpiece.

Since we are cutting a shaped piece with curves in it, the table fence cannot be used and is therefore removed.

With most tables, this automatically removes the guards and the dust extractor connection, but this deficiency can be remedied with a simple home-made device which provides both guard and dust extraction take-off.

This is the same device as used in my edge-moulding article, *see page 105*, and is easily made from batten and transparent plastic. The hole for the dust extractor spout is cut with a hole saw or a home-made small circle cutter.

One further requirement is some kind of lead-in device to enable the workpiece to be gently introduced to the rotating cutter. A plain metal pin is commonly used, but an efficient alternative is a length of batten with a rounded end.

The cutter is set so that the bearing runs on the edge of the pattern, the blades spanning the thickness of the workpiece.

With the router inverted in the table, the direction of rotation of the cutter as we look down on it is anti-clockwise. We therefore rotate the workpiece in an anti-clockwise direction in order to cut against the rotation of the cutter.

Rotating in a clockwise direction is likely to result – with dire consequences – in the workpiece being whipped out of our hands.

Shaping

When shaping the shield, as shown in *photo 2*, the pattern is run against the bearing, enabling the cutter to cut the workpiece exactly to the shape and size of the pattern.

The workpiece need not be pushed hard against the cutter. A light, controlled pass gives the best results – and you can always go round once again to produce a fine finish.

Photo 4 *Intricate pattern being followed with a thin (⅜in) flush trimmer*

Photo 5 *Base pattern for Bosch 1700 ACE being made in 9mm MDF. The router sole plate is used as the original pattern*

Guards and goggles

In some of the photographs shown here, guards have been omitted for the sake of clarity. NEVER on any account use these methods without adequate guards and eye protection. If working with MDF wear a face mask and use dust extraction.

In photo 8 dust extraction is omitted for photographic clarity, but if used its efficiency will be reduced because the router base is hanging over the edge of the workpiece, with consequent drop in vacuum.

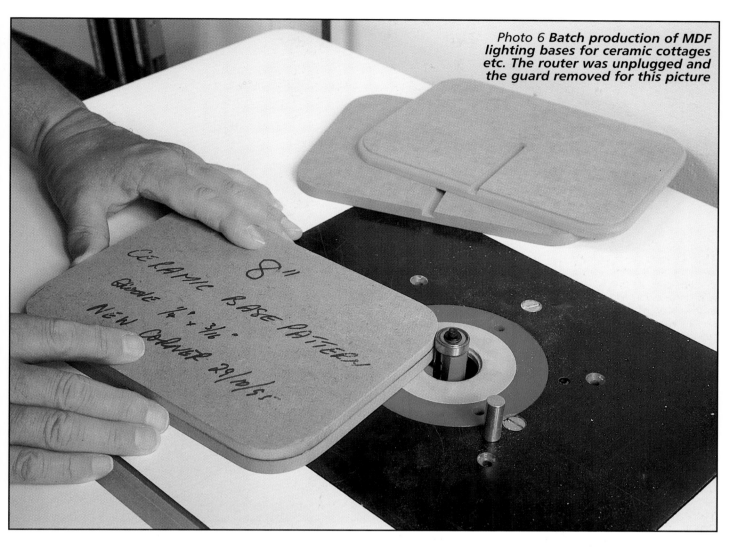

"The hardest part of the job is usually separating the pattern and work-piece after the cut is completed"

The job is completed by separating the pattern and the workpiece with a knife, as shown in *photo 3*.

Flush-trimming cutters come in a wide range of sizes. For intricate shaping operations the thin cutters are particularly useful as they can follow tighter curves. An example is shown, *see photo 4*, in which an intricate pattern is being cut with the C.M.T. ⅜in flush trimmer.

The pattern is for a WoodRat mitre box, *see photo 1*. An even thinner version of the flush trimmer is available from Wealden Cutters. Treat such cutters with care, and take light cuts.

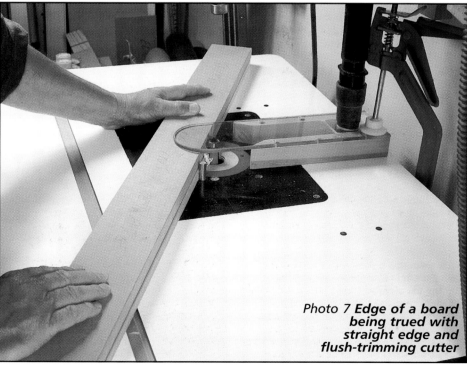

Photo 7 **Edge of a board being trued with straight edge and flush-trimming cutter**

Photo 8 Side of kitchen cabinet being copied, using first side as a pattern

Router base

The techniques used in the above example lend themselves to the making of a pattern for the base of your router, using the plastic sole plate as your master.

Shaping a base pattern will facilitate the making of numerous simple work aids to make your router even more versatile.

Using the black plastic sole plate as the original, a base pattern can be made for the Bosch 1700 ACE (*see photo 5*).

I make MDF bases for ceramic cottages, watermills etc. made by a friend. These are used to provide illumination by fixing a light fitting, flex and plug, and standing the building on its appropriate-size base (*see photo 6*).

A particularly useful application for those who do not have a planer is the truing of board edges or the reduction of width to match a narrower board. All that is necessary is a suitable straight edge taped to the required line of cut.

The workpiece is run past the cutter with the straight edge running against the bearing. The workpiece is cut back to the exact line of the straight edge (*see photo 7*).

Hand-held routing

The kind of repetitive pattern routing considered in this chapter is best done with the router set in a table, especially when dealing with small, curved shapes.

In principle, a hand-held router can be used, the problem of holding the workpiece being solved admirably by use of a table, enabling the work to be held with your own two hands.

Planing of board edges is easily accomplished in this manner. The straight edge is taped to the board as before and the assembly is clamped to the edge of the bench or Workmate.

A top-mounted bearing type of cutter is best for this application, in which the work is clamped to the bench with the pattern (straight edge) uppermost.

A useful application if you are not too sure of the accuracy of your sawing is found when making carcasses for kitchen cabinets from man-made materials such as Contiplas.

If a number of sides of exactly the same size are required you can take pains with the first one and then use this as your pattern, taping it to each rough-cut subsequent panel. I use this method with the profile-guide cutter, pattern uppermost.

A panel is shown being trimmed in this way in *photo 8 (and see Guards and Goggles panel on page 108).*

Copy and keep

When you have achieved a satisfactory pattern, use it to make a perfect copy before you make anything else. Label the copy, with details of its purpose and the cutter used, and put it away in a safe place in case you have a mishap with your original pattern.

If you plan to make many copies it might be worth considering replicating your pattern onto a more durable material such as Tufnol.

Fine **cuts**

Using miniature cutters to rout mini-mouldings for dolls' houses

DOLLS' house makers, modellers and other miniaturists gain great satisfaction from making their projects entirely from scratch, including all the mouldings and miniature components. Until fairly recently it was necessary to make up special scratch stocks to painstakingly produce 1/12 scale skirting boards, picture rails, sash bars, cornices, architraves and the like, but several cutter suppliers now offer miniature replicas of the most popular moulding cutters.

These cutters enable a wide range of shapes to be created with the router, and give the miniaturist control over all stages of the project. The range of miniature cutters now available includes not only the 1/12 scale doll's house variety but also smaller versions of some of the most popular standard cutters such as Roman ogee, Classic ogee, roundover, and ovolo. These are invaluable for putting delicate edges on small items such as jewellery and trinket boxes, hand mirrors, and clock cases.

"Tiny items in a coarse-grained wood just do not look right"

Precision

Miniature work is essentially table work. The secret is care and precision at every

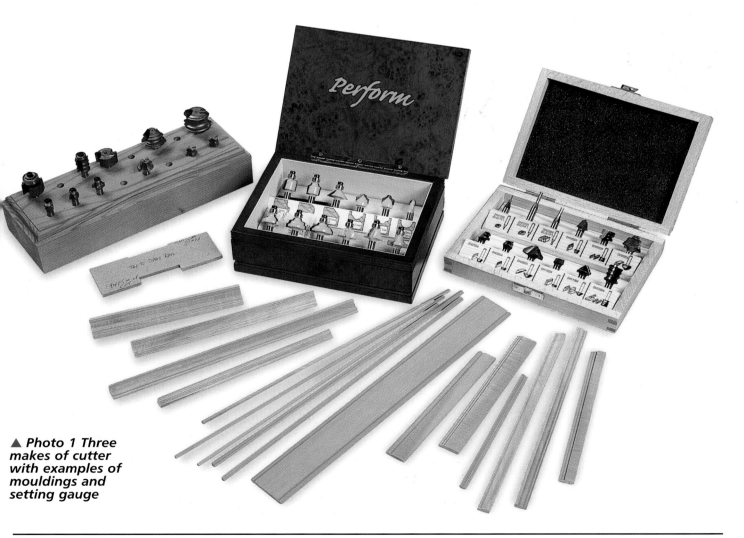

▲ *Photo 1 Three makes of cutter with examples of mouldings and setting gauge*

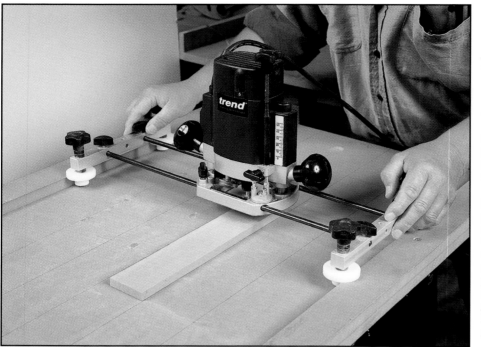

◀ *(Above)* **Photo 2** *A board being thicknessed on my home-made thicknessing table with a T5 router, fine height adjuster and pivot jig parts ...*

◀ *(Below)* **Photo 3** *... similar shot but with a Bosch 1700ACE router on home-made skis*

stage: the selection of the timber, its preparation to exact thickness, the accurate setting of the depth of cut and the table fence, and very careful machining.

The choice of timber is all-important in miniature work. Tiny items in a coarse-grained wood just do not look right, as well as being much harder to work. The best wood is a mild fine-grained hardwood, which will cut cleanly and take the degree of detail required. My favourite for this purpose is jelutong (*Dyer costulata*), but I have also had good results with lime (*Tilia vulgaris*) and obeche (Triplochiton scleroxylon), and there are a number of other fine-grained non-endangered species.

"The boards are sometimes far too thin for passing over a planer by hand"

Timber preparation

Most mouldings will be made on the edge of a board and parted off afterwards. It is crucial that the boards should be prepared to the exact thickness required. You cannot afford to be 1mm out in a 3mm board. If your planing skills are somewhat lacking, the router can be used on 'skis' with the

▼ *(Left)* **Photo 4** *Cutters suitable for thicknessing – CMT dado cutters, Wealden rebate cutter and surface trim cutters*

▼ *(Below)* **Photo 5** *Four pieces of jelutong prepared to specific thicknesses. The figures give the thickness in mm*

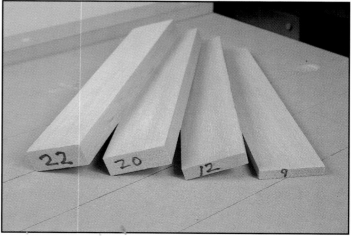

▲ **Photo 6** *The table set-up, with auxiliary fence fitted and Perles OF808 installed. Wealden T6690 cutter. Note hold-downs reversed to clear auxiliary fence*

board held to a flat surface and a bottom-cutting cutter fitted to the router.

If you happen to own a Trend pivot jig, one of its four main modes of work is this very operation. The board is trued on one side, then turned over and gradually skimmed down to the desired thickness. A fine adjuster for depth of cut is almost essential for this kind of work.

I find that a useful mixture of planing and routing is provided by first planing a true face and two square edges on the board, then taping the board face-side down on my home-made thicknessing table and skimming the upper side to the required thickness. The boards are sometimes far too thin for passing over a planer by hand – I always use a home-made safety push-block made from a plastic float trowel covered with a piece of router mat.

Photo 2 shows the thicknessing process on my home-made thicknessing table, using the Trend T5 router, fitted with fine height adjuster, and parts of the Trend pivot jig. *Photo 3* shows the same operation, but with the Bosch 1700 ACE router on home-made skis.

Photo 4 shows a selection of cutters suitable for thicknessing, including CMT dado cutters, a Wealden rebate cutter with bearing removed, and Wealden surface trim cutters.

Photo 5 shows four boards of jelutong prepared to specific thicknesses. Each board is labelled with its thickness in millimetres.

▼ **Photo 7** *Setting gauge being used to set height of cut*

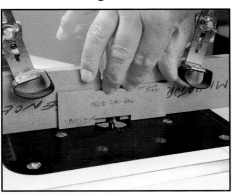

Gauge used to set depth of cut

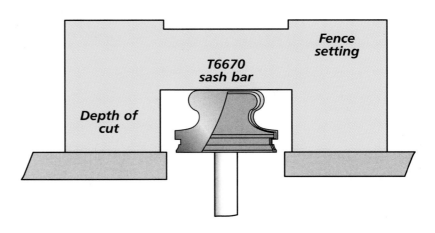

Gauge used to set fence position

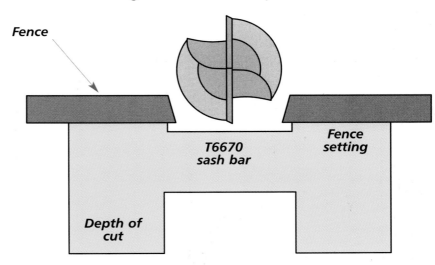

▲ **Fig 1** *Depth of cut and fence-setting gauges*

▼ **Fig 2** *The set up for routing a sash bar*

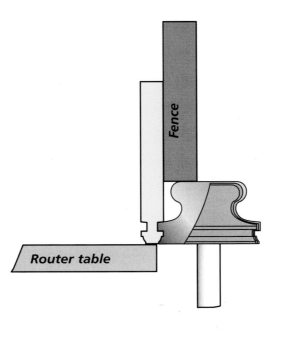

◀ **(Above) Photo 8** *Sash bar being machined in jelutong. Second cut on edge of 3mm board. Wealden T6670 cutter. Note use of safety push block*

◀ **(Below) Photo 9** *Sash bar moulded on the edges of a 3mm board. Finished sash bars parted from the board*

Producing the mouldings

Having prepared the board, the required moulding is run off on the edge, then sawn off. Established miniaturists will use a small fine-toothed circular saw for this; I used a large Startrite bandsaw followed by careful hand sanding.

To produce miniature mouldings, a router table is virtually essential. Most commercial tables have fences with too large a cutter aperture in them, so an auxiliary fence with an aperture cut to match the size of the cutter is required. My auxiliary fences are made of 12mm MDF and simply fastened to the existing fence with double-sided tape. Hold-downs, push-sticks and push-blocks are other essentials.

Neither the table nor the router in it has to be big and powerful. I used the budget system I described earlier (see page 60) with the addition of a fine height adjuster, to cut the mouldings. *Photo 6* shows the table with auxiliary fence fitted, and the Perles OF808 installed.

For those who do not already possess a router table, a very useful booklet is supplied with the Trend set of cutters which, among other things, gives instructions for building a suitable table. The booklet is also available separately from the Trend publications department.

With cutters as small as these it is a

"Neither the table nor the router in it has to be big and powerful"

▶ **Photo 10** *Trend DH 04 Victorian bull-nose with skirting produced with it, plus the Trend DH 06 multi-mould cutter with cornice and architrave produced with it*

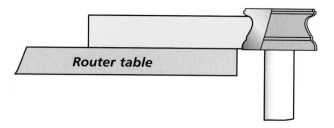

▲ Fig 3 *Picture rails are created by moulding the end of a board first ...*

▼ Fig 4 *... then the board is set vertically to complete*

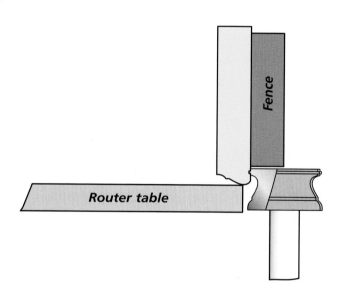

good idea to make the settings with the aid of a magnifying glass. Test cuts will be required, but having achieved the correct settings for depth of cut and position of fence you can make simple gauges for height of cut and fence setting. *Figure 1* shows such a gauge for the Wealden sash bar cutter T6670, and *photo 7* shows a similar gauge for the dado rail cutter T6690 being used to set the height of cut.

The cutters

The cutters shown are from the Axminster, Trend and Wealden ranges. All of these are on ¼in shanks, although the Trend set is also available on 8mm shanks.

The Axminster set consists of miniature versions of standard cutters, although they also produce a 12-piece boxed set of dolls' house cutters. The Trend and Wealden cutters are 1/12 scale dolls' house cutters; those from Trend come in a 12-piece boxed set while the Wealden ones are listed and sold individually.

"Mini-cutters should be kept clean, but not honed for fear of spoiling the detail"

▼ Photo 11 *Axminster miniature Roman ogee cutter with cutter storage block moulded with it*

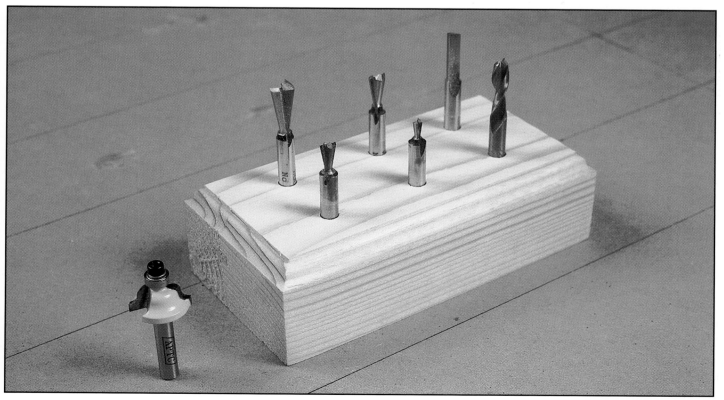

▼ *Photo 12 Thin boards moulded with Axminister miniature cutters, compared with thicker edges moulded with standard cutters*

Dolls' house cutters

The Trend and Wealden ranges include cutters for producing architrave, hand rail, sash bar, dado rail, picture rail, picture frame, cornice and stair-tread nosings. In addition, both suppliers offer very narrow straight cutters and multi-profile cutters (Trend call the latter 'multi-mould') which, by selecting various parts of the profile, can be used to produce many different sections.

All are accurately ground to 1/12 scale, and all are made of TCT. Some of them are very small with intricate detail, so they should be used and stored with great care. They should be kept clean, but not honed for fear of spoiling the detail.

The standard approach for moulding is to run the prepared board past the cutter to mould the edge, then saw the moulding off. For example, the Wealden sash bar moulding cutter T6670 requires a 3mm board to be run on edge, turned round, and run on the opposite edge.

Figure 2 shows the set up, and *photo 8* shows the sash bar being machined. After machining, sand very lightly to remove fluff but don't blur the detail in the moulding. *Photo 9* shows finished mouldings on both edges of a 3mm board, together with some examples of the sawn-off sash bar.

A second example is provided by the Wealden picture rail cutter T6695. This cutter requires a 6mm board and two passes: one with the board flat on the table and one with it on edge with the depth of cut reset (*see figs 3 and 4*). Note that both cuts are made before the moulding is sawn off the board.

A third example is provided by the Trend DH 04 Victorian bull-nose cutter with which I have made a length of skirting board, and as a final example we can take the Trend DH 06 multi-profile cutter. From the wide variety of mouldings that it is capable of, I have made a cornice and an architrave. These are all shown, together with the cutters, in *photo 10*. With cutters such as this, it is a good idea to keep specimens of each moulding you produce to help setting up for a repeat run. You will be constantly finding new shapes and sizes.

Axminster miniature cutters

This is a very interesting set of twelve cutters, consisting of miniature versions of standard moulding cutters. These will find a number of uses in dolls' house work, but are also excellent for decorating the edges of jewellery boxes, clock cases and small cabinets. As with the other cutters, all are of TCT and all but three are bearing guided.

Unlike the other cutters, however, these can be used in a hand-held router, as is evidenced by the bearings. Nevertheless, for simple mouldings I would use them in a table-mounted router where possible, leaving the bearings on and aligning the table fence with the bearing. Timber selection and preparation is important, as usual, but not quite as critical as when making 1/12 scale mouldings.

Photo 11 shows a small cutter storage block with its edges moulded with the miniature Roman ogee cutter.

Photo 12 shows two thin boards with edges moulded with two more of the Axminster cutters. Two thicker boards with edges moulded with standard cutters are also shown for comparison.

"Keep specimens of each moulding you produce to help setting up for a repeat run"

Not much time for gardening: Ron's slant on the window box

METRIC/IMPERIAL CONVERSION CHART

mm	in	mm	in	mm	in	mm	in
1	0.03937	27	1.06299	80	3.14960	340	13.38582
2	0.07874	28	1.10236	90	3.54330	350	13.77952
3	0.11811	29	1.14173	100	3.93700		
4	0.15748	30	1.18110			360	14.17322
5	0.19685			110	4.33070	370	14.56692
		31	1.22047	120	4.72440	380	14.96063
6	0.23622	32	1.25984	130	5.11811	390	15.35433
7	0.27559	33	1.29921	140	5.51181	400	15.74803
8	0.31496	34	1.33858	150	5.90551		
9	0.35433	35	1.37795			410	16.14173
10	0.39370			160	6.29921	420	16.53543
		36	1.41732	170	6.69291	430	16.92913
11	0.43307	37	1.45669	180	7.08661	440	17.32283
12	0.47244	38	1.49606	190	7.48031	450	17.71653
13	0.51181	39	1.53543	200	7.87401		
14	0.55118	40	1.57480			460	18.11023
15	0.59055			210	8.26771	470	18.50393
		41	1.61417	220	8.66141	480	18.89763
16	0.62992	42	1.65354	230	9.05511	490	19.29133
17	0.66929	43	1.69291	240	9.44881	500	19.68504
18	0.70866	44	1.73228	250	9.84252		
19	0.74803	45	1.77165				
20	0.78740			260	10.23622		
		46	1.81102	270	10.62992		
21	0.82677	47	1.85039	280	11.02362		
22	0.86614	48	1.88976	290	11.41732		
23	0.90551	49	1.92913	300	11.81102		
24	0.94488	50	1.96850	310	12.20472		
25	0.98425	60	2.36220	320	12.59842		
26	1.02362	70	2.75590	330	12.99212		

1mm = 0.03937in
1cm = 0.3937in
1m = 3.281ft
1in = 25.4mm
1ft = 304.8mm
1yd = 914.4mm

IMPERIAL/METRIC CONVERSION CHART

in		mm	in		mm	in		mm
0	0	0	25/64	0.390625	9.9219	25/32	0.78125	19.8438
1/64	0.015625	0.3969	13/32	0.40625	10.3188	51/64	0.796875	20.2406
1/32	0.03125	0.7938	27/64	0.421875	10.7156	13/16	0.8125	20.6375
3/64	0.046875	1.1906	7/16	0.4375	11.1125	53/64	0.828125	21.0344
1/16	0.0625	1.5875	29/64	0.453125	11.5094	27/32	0.84375	21.4312
5/64	0.078125	1.9844	15/32	0.46875	11.9062	55/64	0.858375	21.8281
3/32	0.09375	2.3812	31/64	0.484375	12.3031	7/8	0.875	22.2250
7/64	0.109375	2.7781	1/2	0.500	12.700	57/64	0.890625	22.6219
1/8	0.125	3.1750	33/64	0.515625	13.0969	29/32	0.90625	23.0188
9/64	0.140625	3.5719	17/32	0.53125	13.4938	59/64	0.921875	23.4156
5/32	0.15625	3.9688	35/64	0.546875	13.8906	15/16	0.9375	23.8125
11/64	0.171875	4.3656	9/16	0.5625	14.2875	61/64	0.953125	24.2094
3/16	0.1875	4.7625	37/64	0.578125	14.6844	31/32	0.96875	24.6062
13/64	0.203125	5.1594	19/32	0.59375	15.0812	63/64	0.984375	25.0031
7/32	0.21875	5.5562	39/64	0.609375	15.4781			
15/64	0.234375	5.9531	5/8	0.625	15.8750			
1/4	0.250	6.3500	41/64	0.640625	16.2719			
17/64	0.265625	6.7469	21/32	0.65625	16.6688			
9/32	0.28125	7.1438	43/64	0.671875	17.0656			
19/64	0.296875	7.5406	11/16	0.6875	17.4625			
5/16	0.3125	7.9375	45/64	0.703125	17.8594			
21/64	0.1328125	8.3344	23/32	0.71875	18.2562			
11/32	0.34375	8.7312	47/64	0.734375	18.6531			
23/64	0.359375	9.1281	3/4	0.750	19.0500			
3/8	0.375	9.5250	49/64	0.765625	19.4469			

1in = 1.000 = 25.40mm

ABOUT THE AUTHOR

Ron Fox has been involved with routing since his school days. He built his own workshop at 16, referring to it as 'the boathouse' to avoid local planning regulations. Over the years he has amassed a huge collection of hand tools and woodworking machinery, in the process gaining a wide-ranging experience and a vast practical knowledge.

In 1990 he negotiated an early retirement to pursue his woodturning interests full time. A few years later he found himself running routing courses, and this is still a major part of his woodworking life despite becoming increasingly involved with writing articles for woodworking magazines.

Ron has been a guest demonstrator at two Woodcut Exhibitions and gave the Routing Masterclass at the annual International Woodworking Exhibition in 1998, 1999 and 2000. He also works in an advisory capacity and is often asked to test new cutters and suggest design corrections. This puts him in the privileged position of being able to put his hands on almost any item of routing equipment. Despite this, he is a firm believer in making simple work aids and gadgets.

INDEX

acetone 35
aluminium, cutters for 24
ambient air cleaners 53
anti-tilt plates 26, 91
AquaVac Synchro 30A 51, 62
arbor-mounted cutters 7–8
'Astonish' cleaner 9, 13
Axminster Power Tool Centre 36

base plates 3–4
bearing-guided cutters
    grooved cuts 20
    honing 14
    setting depths of cut 19
biscuit jointing 48
Bosch RT60 router table 44, 45
box-maker's jigs 59
boxed sets of cutters 8–9, 62–5
breakout 26, 28–9
budget equipment, basic kit 60–5
burn 26, 29, 87

Charnwood W002 router table 65
Chesterman Marketing 34
circle jigs 104–5
circles
    cutting techniques 30–1, 103–5
    direction of cut 23, 30–1
Circular sub-base (Trend) 81
clamps 33–4
cleaning
    cutters 9, 12–13
    diamond hones 14
climb-cutting see reverse cuts
clothing for work safety 56
collets 3, 4
    maintenance 15–16
'Craftsman' router table (Trend) 44, 45
curves, cutting techniques 101–3
Cutter and Collet Care (Trend) 16
cutter blocks 15
cutter speed 24
cutters
    basic types 6–8
    bearing-guided 14, 19, 20
    boxed sets 8–9, 62–5
    flush trimming 48, 109
    for aluminium 24
    for freehand work 85
    for miniature work 111, 115–16

for Perspex 24
long-reach 69, 81
maintenance 9, 11–14, 24
safety 58
single cutters 9, 65
storage 15, 24
cutting boards for vacuum tables 36
cutting direction 22–3
    circles 23, 30–1
    curves 101–2
    freehand work 87
    pattern routing 108
    reverse cuts 26, 27–31
cutting jig 88, 92
cutting tables 71–6

depth of cut 4, 17–19, 47–8
    see also fine height adjusters
diamond hones 9, 13
    cleaning 14
direction of cut 22–3
    circles 23, 30–1
    curves 101–2
    freehand work 87
    reverse cuts 26, 27–31
    pattern routing 108
dolls' house cutters 116
door frame rails, scribing 48
double-sided tape 34
dovetailing 31, 38, 79
down-cutting see reverse cuts
drilling bases 90
dust extraction 4, 5, 49–53, 57, 62

E-Z HOLD
    bar clamps 33, 36
edge distance 19–20
edge mouldings, rippling 26, 29–30
electrical safety 54–5
end grain breakout 26, 29
end grain burn 26, 29

F-clamps 34
false bases 90
false fences 88–9
Festo 'Basic Plus' router table 44, 45
fine adjusters, side fences 5, 19–20
fine height adjusters 4, 19, 37–41
    home-made 41
    see also depth of cut

fire precautions 55, 56
fixed speed routers 3
floors in workshops 55–6
flush trimming cutters 48, 109
Formica lippings, trimming 30
freehand routing
    basic technique 82–7
    dust extraction 52–3
    routers for 3

grooved cuts 20
guidebushes 5, 77–80
    working techniques 67–70

handles on routers 4
handscrews 34, 36
Hard to Find Tools 34, 36
high speed steel (HSS) cutters 6
Hitachi M6SB laminate trimmer 83
holding workpieces 32–6
    freehand work 85–6
hones 9, 13
    cleaning 14
honing techniques 9, 13–14
hot melt glue guns 35, 36
housing jig 88, 92
housings, breakout 29
HSS (high speed steel) cutters 6

interchangability of fine height
    adjusters 39–41
ISD router tables 44

jigs
    box maker's 59
    circle 104–5
    cutting 88, 92
    dovetail 31, 79
    housing 88, 92
    trimming 88, 92
John Mills Ltd 36
jointing cutters 7
Jorgensen
    E-Z HOLD bar clamps 33, 36
    handscrews 34, 36

Klemmsia cam clamps 33–4, 36

laminate trimming routers 83
laminates, trimming 30

Leigh dovetail jig 31, 79
lighting for work 56, 86
lippings, trimming 30
Lo-Tec Pieman 36
long-reach cutters 69, 81

M. Power Tools Ltd 36
material
    freehand work 85, 87
    miniature work 112–13
Microclene ambient air cleaners 53
Microclene Filters Ltd 53
Mini-Mach vacuum table 36, 86
miniature cutters 111, 115–6
miniature work, techniques 111–16
motor power 2–3
moulded edges, finishing 26, 29–30

nail varnish remover 35

panel raising 48
parallel guides see side fences
pattern routing 106–10
Perles OF 808 router 61
personal safety gear 56–7, 108
    freehand work 86
Perspex, cutters for 24
plunge legs 3
pocket cutters see cutters, long-reach
poor-quality cuts 25
problems
    breakout 26, 28–9
    burn 26, 29, 87
    poor-quality cuts 25
    rippling of edge mouldings 26,
        29–30
    run-in/run-out 25–6, 88
    tilt 26, 91
PTFE-based sprays 9, 13
pushing v pulling 23

Quick Grip clamps 33

Racal Airlite respirator 56–7
rate of feed 24
rebates, getting clean edges 28
Record G-clamps 33
Record RPR60T table 44
respirators 56–7
reverse cuts 26, 28–9, 31

rippling of edge mouldings 26, 29–30
router bases, pattern making 110
router mats 36
router tables 43–8, 65
    dust extraction 52
    making 45–6, 114
    miniature work 114
    routers suitable for 4, 47–8
routers
    components and buying 2–5, 61
    for freehand work 3, 82–3
    for table work 4, 47–8
    safe use of 57–9
routing equipment, budget kit 60–5
'Routrack' tables (Trend) 44
run-in/run-out problem 25–6, 88

sacrificial boards for vacuum tables 36
safety 54–9, 108
sash bar mouldings 48
Saw Doctors Association 14
scribing door frame rails 48
shank diameter of cutters 8
shaping cutters 6–7
side fences 4, 5
    fine adjusters 5, 19–20
single-handed clamps 33
Solo single-handed clamps 33
spiral cutters, maintenance 14
spraying of cutters 9, 13
storage of cutters 15, 25
straight cutters 6
straight guides see side fences
sub-bases 69, 81
suppliers' addresses
    Axminster Power Tool Centre 36
    Hard to Find Tools 36
    John Mills Ltd 36
    Lo-Tec Pieman 36
    M. Power Tools Ltd 36
    Microclene Filters Ltd 53
    Trend Machinery and Cutting
        Tools Ltd 36
switches on routers 4–5

table inserts 45, 48
tables see cutting tables; router tables
tape, double-sided 34
TCT (tungsten-carbide-tipped)
    cutters 6

templates 68, 70
tenon cutting 48
tilt 26, 91
timber
    freehand work 85, 87
    miniature work 112–13
Titman router table 44
toggle clamps 34, 36
trammel bars 100–4
Trend Machinery and Cutting
    Tools Ltd 36
Trend Routing Catalogue 67
trimming cutters 6
trimming jig 88, 92
trimming laminates and lippings 30
tungsten-carbide-tipped (TCT)
    cutters 6

Unibase (Trend) 81
up-cutting 28

V-Mach vacuum table 36
vacuum tables 36
variable speed routers 2–3
Veritas
    router jack 39
    router table 44, 59
vernier gauges 19
ViseGrip clamps 33

WD40 9, 12–13
weights for holding work 32
wood
    freehand work 85, 87
    miniature work 112–13
Woodcut Trading Company
    999-200 table 65
    table insert 45, 48
WoodRat PlungeBar 39, 47, 65
work clothing 56
Workmates 32
workpieces, holding devices for
    hand routing 32–6
workshop safety 55–6
wrong-way cuts see reverse cuts

Zyliss vice 34, 36